Heading for Home

Dear Jonathon

Through you I have learned and been able to experience good practice.

(The chapter on Bulls & Essence of Ranching within has some of the other)

We have shared values.

This book is to say a big thank you

Zahava

Zahava Hanan **Heading for Home**

How beautiful upon the mountains are the feet of him that bringeth good tidings. Isaiah LII, 7.

Each day at Rumsey…	8	Prologue
As I go to my secret spot…	10	Grandfather Nahum
The creek that runs through…	12	My Father
Speckles of snow are falling…	18	The Sacred and the Profane
	20	
	25	
April's end…	28	Rumsey
The whirr of wings…	32	Meeting the Land
I come this morning…	35	Jim Commodore
	45	
Yesterday I arrived…	51	Bulls
Bucky came to the ranch…	55	Andy Russell
Winter is swapping-story time…	58	Breakfast at Rumsey Ranch
The feverish scurry and flurry…	70	The Essence of Ranching
Before the break of day…	74	Fresh Tracks
	80	Foot of Man and Hoof of Beast
	82	
	90	
	93	
	96	
	101	
	112	
	114	
	122	
	124	

This book is dedicated to Samuel, Milt & Alan: three wise men.

To all those who have encircled me with love in the writing of this book I give my gratitude: in Canada my dear friend David Wood, and in England Lord Esher, Sir Rodney Touche, the Hon. Sir Jonathon Porritt and John Bush, all gave help in keeping me on track beyond anything one should expect from one's friends.

And I thank too my ancestors.

Z. H.

Prologue

My heart always leaps when I reach Rumsey; entering it I see a view into infinity, and feel that I am going into protecting hills which will surround and comfort me. Returning to my Garden of Paradise, I am acutely conscious of being happy. We all, somewhere, have our own idea of earthly Paradise, be it a tropical island or a bleak landscape where no one lives.

Water is abundant on my ranch, for there are several natural wells of springing water, and a mile and a half of creek wanders through. Walking alongside this creek, whose source is the mountain water that tumbles with happiness in the spring; knowing it through seasons when the weather has beauty and gentleness, and others when it can be daunting; seeing it when the grass along its edge scarcely stirs, or when it is flooded with wind, fills me with a joy that never dies.

We did not think of the great open plains, the beautiful rolling hills, and the winding streams with tangled growth as wild.
Only to the white man was nature a wilderness…to us it was tame.
The Earth was beautiful, and we were surrounded with blessings of the great mystery.
Chief Luther Standing Bear, Sioux

The rolling hills that were beautiful to the first people are now my Paradise, and I too feel "surrounded with blessings of the great mystery". Whatever happens, it is important that one's faith in goodness is not taken away.

Rumsey, viewed from afar, lies in the eternal foothills of Alberta, with nests of time manifested in the buffalo bones and in the occasional tools dating back 4,000 years which turn up in the earth during ploughing, linking us in the present with an Indian encampment that existed then.

White man's adaptation to this country, and to the herds of domestic animals that sustain him there, shows first in the landscapes with their log barns and barbed wire fences. God's earth, which supported buffalo, elk, deer, and the first Native people, had a shift in its population, with the white man forcing the Natives into reservations and buffaloes pushed off the face of the earth. In their stead the Europeans brought the cow, and people to herd and take care of the cow, some good men, some not so good.

Below this patch of earth were the blessings of the deep; below this patch of sky, the blessings of Heaven. My father tried to cherish the plants within his crop and the animals of his stock as best he knew. To the Jew, aware from his Biblical learnings of the invisible presence of the Creator everywhere, God in his holiness was in every living creature and plant, and in this ministration of earth's surface the kindness of God was felt. There was no abrupt separation between reverence for the land and living creatures and the need to earn a living: the one flowed out of the other. Harmony and rhythm are qualities that do not normally fit into the business world, and it is sometimes difficult for entrepreneurs to keep in mind that there is an ethical approach to life.

Late one afternoon in June I was walking in the foothills of my grazing land, perceiving my sacred surroundings, with nature's carpet of buffalo beans at my feet, three-pointed aven, tiny everlasting pussyfoots, hairy picune, incense, wild delphinium and wild violets — earth-time with its inner clocks and the succession of plants that spring up. I had missed the crocus, but I had the further outsprouting and upwelling to look forward to, the wild roses to come and go, the yarrow, bluebells, golden rod and purple asters yet to arise.

Away from highways, I was glad of any reason for continuing my journey by cow paths, elk paths and horse trails. Out on the range the Garden of Eden freshness was like something I had never breathed before. I inhaled the sweet fragrance of the grasslands that in primordial time the buffaloes too had walked on, and the goodness of being alive met me in a moment. I was sharing my walk with elk, observing how they snatch delicious bites as they travel. In bringing my cattle to meet these grasslands along with the elk, I know that this balance cannot truly exist unless I become a caretaker of this earth whilst I am here. Always, whether with summer grazing or growing hay feed for winter, it is a necessity that my land should be in good heart. How grateful I feel that in the course of my work I meet the earth.

Let this book be a journey into a landscape and its people and the creatures thereon. Let us travel slowly, for, as with a herd and young calves, if men should overdrive all the herd will die. So I will lead you softly on, according to the pace of the cattle.

Each day at Rumsey ranch succeeded the other in a carefree routine. Standing on the side, thinking of the Earth's clock, I was aware of three other circles of time intertwining in my life.

One circle was the cyclical division of the year for the purposes of the ranch. It was Cosmic time, concerned with the management of the land and the herd, when to put the bulls with the cows and when to pull the bulls from the cows.

The second circle was my own human destiny sauntering hopefully to the music of time and hearing its secret harmonies.

The third concerned the Plant on my grazing land which was owned by Big Oil, and which became part of our concern in running the ranch well. Their pace was not for everybody; it was industry time, far less relaxed – in fact, astonishingly restless. There is a Western singer called Stompin' Tom whose foot slaps and taps at the floor, using it as if it were a drum, wearing out many a shoe sole. That, for me, evoked their sphere of time.

Whilst the oil business was unfolding itself, I took to walking towards the woods and to looking at the creek. I remember one lengthening March twilight with pine trees dark and distant, and the embers of a serenely cloudy sky towering over me, both transitory and yet eternal; it was then that I began spontaneously to saunter to what became my secret spot, and from this moment my free-wheeling walk became an essential element of my life. What need was there to worry or enter into their frets and threats and huffiness when my whole being felt and knew that it was part of some great chord of music? All the wonder to be discovered exists inside each one of us. I would emerge always from my gentle revisitations as refreshed as dew-soaked grass.

Walking through the tree gateway to my secret spot, and looking at the creek on the way, I was, I suppose, seeking after truth. The currents in the creek were always there, and yet at each moment they were composed of different elements. It changed unceasingly; only the direction of its motion was unchanged. I could see it, feel it, but never comprehend it. In the end all thought must end in awe before the mystery of the unknowable.

So whenever I needed to be alone I went with my dog Bucky to my secret spot, where no one ever came but the two of us — though latterly Willow, my cat, not to be left out, often came too.

Our travels there took us on foot over terrain that included a patch of hayfield, a creek crossing, native pastures, and over the foothills up to the moose run where snowy mountain-tops could be seen, and a high ridge with Engelman spruce, a variety that appeared nowhere else on the ranch. Elk and moose trod the lovely, narrow paths. In spring I could smell the resin and fir needles, and sap oozed from the trunks where elk had scratched for it when the snow was on the ground.

As these walkabouts meandered their way through the year, by interspersing my remembrances of them through this book I have tried to compose for the reader a simple way of tip-toeing with me to my Source of influence; to reveal secret things; and to share the mysteries of my heart.

The Lord hath his way in the whirlwind and in storm, and the clouds are the dust of his feet.
Prophet Nahum

Grandfather Nahum

This story should begin with my grandfather Nahum.

If one were to ask an old cattleman which was the best winter he had ever experienced in Alberta, he would scratch his head and ponder irresolutely, because he would think of so many good ones; but if he were asked which were the worst, he would remember keenly and say 1886-7 and 1906-7.[1] The winter of '86 was a terrible one, with snow piling all over the country in deep, crusted drifts, blizzards screaming across the open, cattle humping up and perishing from the bitter cold. It was without doubt the worst winter ever seen in the Alberta ranch business, for, although the loss was heavier in 1906-7, there were circumstances leading up to the earlier winter that accentuated the inclemency of weather. Everything seemed to conspire to place range stock at a disadvantage, and the results were tremendous losses.

Fall started poorly, with late rains, frozen, uncured grasses, and early cold. Prairie fires and crowded ranges took the grass off and left little for winter rustling – in fact, in some districts the range was so depleted that the cattle went into winter in very poor condition, even hay being insufficient to strengthen them against the cold. Mange made some stock even more susceptible, for, with impoverished bodies, the animals could not resist the inroads of parasites, and by New Year numbers of cattle were hairless. So it was that lack of food, poor condition, exceptional storms, and snow and cold took a fearful toll of the range stock.

One day in January 1887 the citizens of Macleod saw what appeared to be a low, black cloud above the snow to the north. The cloud drew slowly, draggingly nearer, until it was seen that a herd of thousands of range cattle were coming from the north, staggering blindly along the sixty-foot confines of the road in search of open places where they could feed. A steady, piteous moaning filled the air as the creatures drew close, feeble, starving, skinned from the knees down by sharp snowcrusts and from stumbling and struggling to rise, hair frozen off in patches - naked, mangy steers, tottering yearlings, and dying cows. Straight into town they crawled, travelling six and eight abreast, bellowing and lowing appeals which no one was able to satisfy. Their numbers were so great that it took over half-an-hour for them to pass a given point. Right through the town they dragged themselves, into the blackness of the prairie beyond, where they were swallowed up and never heard of again, every head being doubtless dead before the week had passed.

Pitiful stories came from everywhere. Starving stock brought in from the range took no interest in the hay before their very noses, standing till they fell over and died; on the range they perished singly, in scores, in hundreds. Not a mile of Canadian Pacific Railway fencing but showed in spring the bodies lying where the fence had barred the drifting, and caused the dazed animals to stand helplessly until the end came. "Ranchers who had not been upset to see dead buffalo everywhere were sickened by what the winter of '86 did to their cattle. Some gave up ranching entirely; some could never own a cow again…The winter of '86 was the end of all but a few of the giant investor-owned ranches."[2]

On the railway tracks the crews, reluctant to crash among them, from pity, and also from fear of damage to the train, decided to chase the animals away. So a brakeman with a lighted lantern was sent to do the chasing, and on one occasion a wild steer proceeded to liven things up by going after the man with so much vigour that a sweep of his horns caught the wire handle of the lantern, tore it from the hand of the fast-departing brakie, and fired the animal's heart with a frenzy of fear. No shaking, bucking or plunging would free the terrible glaring object from where it hung, and the steer broke away on a long gallop, flitting like a gigantic firefly across the expanse of snow. Cowboys saw the strange spectacle, headed it off and drove it into a corral, where they removed the lantern. The lucky steer stayed around the stables and picked up a living through the winter. The lantern is still an object of interest at the Grassy Lake Ranch.

In the Calgary district the loss was estimated at sixty per cent, and in some districts the owners lost practically every head that was at large on the range. For the buffaloes, which are much more forgiving, it was different: where they roamed they fed into the storm or rooted down pretty deep. So they survived.

This was the world my father entered at the age of nine.

My grandfather and his people were mostly scholars steeped in the Hebrew tradition. They came to land that Palliser had designated as uninhabitable. With the holy books which they had carried with them from Russia they lived in holes dug in the earth until they could put up their log cabins. First of my family came my Aunt Ilke, my father's older sister. Brought up near St Petersburg by an uncle who made her his heir, she used the money to emigrate at the age of fifteen to Alberta. To begin with, she brought her two older brothers. Once she had established them she sent for her parents and her younger brother, my father. To her, such behaviour was nothing more than the normal and absolute return of love, the sacred call of the heart.

This was in 1906. When my grandfather arrived, he brought with him old Hebrew books, a Bible and a prayer book. One of the books was entitled How to Create an Inner Temple Without an Outer Temple. A tangible form of doing this was a mezuzah, which he put on the doorpost: a prayer was contained in a cardboard case, with the name of God showing; one kissed it as one went in and out, and this helped to lend a feeling that the entrance of the home was a temple. The prayer shawl he did not wear just for praying, but as a vestment all day long. This loyalty to his inheritance helped him to see everything around him as sacred and eternal, letting the vital flow of continuity of race flow from Adam through him and beyond. Reading these holy books that were worn almost to shreds was a fixed part of each day. He prayed and read harder than anyone I knew in my childhood.

Bunyan's feat was to correlate the long walk which Jesus made through the Holy Land with a typical walk of a seventeenth-century Englishman; my grandfather's feat, homesteading in Rumsey, near Calgary, in a landscape wondrously similar to biblical topography, was to mingle a moral and spiritual map which contained at once Alberta and Israel. And my own trail, which has taken me from Moses and the Wilderness to the forest land east of St. Petersburg and the foothills of Alberta, seemingly is part of a design. Of one thing I am certain – the vision and values of the Prophets are within me.

What was unique for him was that this landscape had no deadly reticence of pain, as the old world had. Some animals and people can feel, as they stand on the earth, where suffering has been. In this new land there was no troubling of the earth's surface where my grandfather stood. And there was freedom from fear; here a man could walk tall, arms outspread, instead of pulling inwards to a self-styled ghetto. The river banks were fringed by a land of silver willow with minute yellow flowers with an overwhelming perfume, emanating at springtime, which is unique to Alberta, and was my father's favourite "scent memory". The trees grew chiefly in gravel beds alongside creeks in a surround of white flowers. The Old Man's Garden (Old Man is the native word for the Creator), with pure soil all through to the depth of the universe, had no echo of ancient barbarities.

Palm branches and lemons, which are symbols in Israel of harvest celebration, were sent to Alberta each year, making a tangible connection between the old world and the new. Each Friday night, after prayers, coins were put in tin boxes for charities in Israel.

My grandfather rode on horseback, teaching Hebrew to his neighbours. Within the bigger town of Calgary the divine was to be found only in the synagogue, and within this urban setting the most spiritual destination that one could head for was the graveyard. But my grandfather's visitation with God was in his daily being and doing, not through synagogue and temple. His journey through life caused his contemplative eyes to become calmer and calmer, looking both inward and outward, revealing his "eternal lineaments", in Blake's words. So this ordinary man's life became a heroic journey, making his homestead at Rumsey shine with the light of heaven itself, and giving him a sacred vitality that lasted until his eighties.

When Nahum died he left Rumsey to his daughter Ilke, for in truth it was hers. My aunt fitted into the tradition of Russian women, who are very generous in spirit, clear in the head and tender in the heart. Childhood memories well up of her garden, which was tended in reverence of growth and awesome in its harvest yield. Everything from it was put away in glass sealers for the winter. Hers was the only home where I saw lettuce preserved and lettuce blinis served, and hers was the joy of harvesting the first wheat crop from Rumsey's virgin soil. Underneath the floor was a root cellar of preserved vegetables and crab apples (Alberta's only domesticated fruit) tucked away for cold winter moments.

To enter her home felt, somehow, as if one were a baby being swaddled in love. Every corner contained photos of cherished relatives. She had beautiful Russian embroidery, mostly worked in red and black cross-stitch, and in true pioneer fashion she added crocheted edges to flour sacks to make tablecloths. There were always lots of potted plants about, most memorably scented geraniums and verbena leaves. Wherever she was, she created an atmosphere of her own, be it in a shelter dug out of the ground, as at the beginning of her life in Canada, in a log cabin, or later in her 90's when she was in hospital.

Aunt Ilke had a fierce energy and a strong will. Until her death she was a powerhouse of energy and commitment, allowing no obstacle to stand in her way. Some people, of whom my mother was one, could not tolerate this quality of intensity, but it appealed to an aspect of myself that is also intense, and she was very dear to me. She also, I think, felt a special tenderness for me, though all her family came under her protection. One of my clearest memories is of going with her to the cemetery before the day of atonement, the holiest day of the year for the special remembering of those nearest to us. With a great flow of feeling she said, "I know I miss my brothers", and after a pause, almost to herself, "Half the family is under the ground".

1. This vivid description of the winters of 1886-7 and 1906-7 is taken, almost verbatim but in a slightly amended form, from *The Range Men* by L.V. Kelly (75th Anniversary Edition, 1988).
2. *Great Plains* by Ian Frazier (Faber and Faber, 1990).

As I go to my secret spot today, January 12th 1993, it is still deep winter, and my journey there is quite daunting. There have been several weeks of 35° – 40° below, and the ice crystals in the creek resemble coral reef. It is like skiing cross-country over a field of crystals. Bucky stops every once in a while to suck the lumps of ice out of his paws. They tinkle just like glass, those little lumps of frozen snow, one against the other.

Even though I skiied along the frozen creek, and Bucky followed coyote tracks that criss-crossed it, when it was time to go home he felt he hadn't had enough fun out of doors, so I thought, "Whatever the obstacles, to the secret spot we must go". But we have to plough through clouds of snow so full that sometimes you can drown in them. Lots of beautiful tracks, although they are more ephemeral today. I find it hard to distinguish between Bucky tracks and coyote tracks, because the wind has blown over them and shifted them.

There are no words to describe the feast for the eyes. But the creek is precarious because some parts are frozen solid and some still flow, and if my foot went in it would be like an instant deep freeze. Moccasins are perfect for snow in these temperatures, but moosehide leather is terrible if it gets wet in 30° below.

It took that depth of chill to freeze the creek and its surrounds into such beauty, and that depth of frost forced me, in the end, to turn back before reaching my secret spot. It was too dangerous to continue. On the way home Bucky was busy digging into a coyote cave with all four paws. Even though the earth is frozen he has made a dent. But they're not there right now – they've moved house, I guess…

January is not always thus. A year later a chinook arch was in the sky and warmth was in the air. You need that depth of cold to have the beauty that comes with the crystallisation of water into snow and ice; and then with such a weather change you can enjoy the beauty without the threat of the windchill. I love the cold that fences you in, that doesn't allow you to go out for fear of death; and then, when a temporary thaw comes, the total immersion of your being in the pure present has a fresh delight.

So on this day, and with this feeling, I decided to lie in the snow; I felt I was lying on a cloud – it was billowing, it moved, it had waves in it, the white clouds in the heaven above were under me. It felt like heaven on earth.

What I knew then was that I had arrived at a still-point; life became an understanding of rhythm – of the world's rhythm and my own rhythm – and an awareness of the importance behind all this of the still-point, where you can never stay but only visit for a moment.

So I rose and went back to work truly revitalised, and took a handful of snow to my lips to complete it.

*He shall be as the light of the morning, when
the sun riseth, even a morning without clouds;
as the tender grass springing out of the earth
by clear shining after rain.*
Samuel II, xxiii, 4

My Father

My father, Samuel Hanan, was named after a famous mystic, and the word "Hanan" comes from the first words of the Hebrew, חנן, meaning the secret science of the Kabala. It also means a state of grace. The name, be it spelled in English Hanan, Hannen, Hanen, Hanin, or Hanina, is often cited in the Bible, Talmud and Midrash, showing by its frequency that the bearers possessed a great store of learning. As in the book of Samuel he too, coming late in the family, was "asked of the Lord".

In the act of personal recollection of my own father I will not retrace his footsteps. I will here make big demands on the reader, leaving the rest to the imaginative side.

Picking a Saskatoon berry this dawn, August 9th 1995, my thoughts drift back to Saskatoon picking in our family. Even in this gathering my father was always standing outside, sculpting a space for himself, choosing to be guardian of his own circle of solitude. There was a paradox of standing outside and yet being committed all the time, as opposed to those who have intensity and are not ever standing outside. He made me conscious of how difficult it is to keep in touch with a sense of self that is separate, within a crowd. A lone flyer amongst a flock of birds is rare: he was that.

Whenever people gathered, be it businessmen or bankers, he always did stand outside and see other layers, other strata, all the streams that bind life together. Although he made friends with the Mammon of unrighteousness, as in the New Testament, that was not what he was after, but he took it into account. In distancing himself from the mechanics of living, he was better able to beam in with an inner sense on the true present. I write of him as if I go to a window to look at the landscape and point out what I see.

Truth mattered to him. Everyone is always wondering in the privacy of their mind and heart what is truth and what is a lie. Good and truth were not abstract concepts to him. His inner perception could think truth and feel goodness. He helped me with that.

My father's roots stemmed from the soil. The idea of a Promised Land is one of the tenets of the Hebrew religion. His passion for land, and his need for it, led him from his father's homestead at Rumsey to own one of the larger ranches in Alberta, his kingdom. The love of proper ploughing and of haymaking was pivotal to his life at Rumsey, but he grew as I did to prefer ranching to farming. He loved to see the wind in a field of grass, or grain ready for harvesting, moving through space with all the rhythm and flow of ocean waves.

He was brought up to know there is divinity in everything, and a non-harming of his fellow creatures was central to his being. He would not kill flies, but would open the door and let them out. Gifts of life come from the earth, and they are given to us all.

The man-animal link is one of the gifts of life, and there was a bond between my father and myself and our link with horses. His horse, Tom, lived on with me. Being given the run of the camp, he survived to be the oldest horse in Alberta at that time, dying at the age of thirty-seven. My own horse was called Izaak – Hebrew for laughter. He died at about the same age as Tom. He was the father of my horse family. Melanie, his wife, had died earlier, and Cloudy, their daughter, is peering out on page 34. When he was down and dying I was kneeling close to him giving him a bit of brandy, for it was very cold. I felt at the moment that everything else was irrelevant, for as he really looked at me I knew I was seeing truth.

Flowing from the perception of God in every creature came concern about human beings. My father was very aware of the existence of others and of what took place between them – a good people-watcher, but not a judge of them. He believed that to try to know a person one must not begin by looking through them. He was self-ambushed behind the mask of a simple man, which he was not. There was a good conscience and a truthfulness, a clarity which is the sign of a wise man.

There are men who are like big trees. Nothing grows under a big tree. My father was not one of them. Those near his tree were nurtured. My best and most meaningful times with him were when we were talking and walking, or sometimes such an intimacy was arrived at during winter darkness and days of mists when it was *rather Russian* to talk about why we were here, and what was it all about anyway.

He taught me the fun and importance of walking barefoot on the earth. The need to do it to toughen up one's soles, and they did toughen up. Once you have the hang of walking, trotting, light but efficient on bare feet, you are more likely to go through life in that way. You cannot go barefoot without being like a child: it is to be in the moment, and to be in the moment in life means being on the beam.

His delicacy of feeling, sense of responsibility and his true listening are traits that have become rare in our times. He was always ready to listen to the schemers and dreamers of Alberta, with their various projects, bringing in lumps of coal and rock with streaks of copper in it, for he was a dreamer himself. But I also remember his close friendships with people of the land, such as Walter Knight, brother of the famous rider, Pete Knight, who came to my father in the middle of the night when Pete was thrown and died.

Through him, too, I learned that the outermost skin does not matter – whether someone is thin or fat or pink with purple spots. When Cezanne was old and shabby and shuffled along, children would jeer and throw stones at him; but his inner being was beautiful, with a glory that he could transform into the singularity of his work.

There was a great sense of silence in his early years, for he knew the nothingness of words. Some men in business can be boastful, but there was understatement with him. He approached everything unaccompanied, inconspicuous and wordless. The attentiveness on my part was engendered by this understatement and reserve.

Looking at the sky always helps. Within his being also was an omnipresent consciousness of the sky. I think my love of sky and skyscapes comes from him. As in the Bible, clouds are looked to for signs. I remember his body quivering as he saw the moon passing behind a cloud. "For the cloud of the Lord was upon the tabernacle by day and fire was on it by night."

He himself never lost his luminous quality. There was a beauty and a love between us that has lit my life and given me strength ever since. There are memories of feelings that have exercised a decisive influence on me. With my father, it was a true meeting. The tone of my life was modified in my thinking, as well as seeing, the world through his eyes. He helped to create a climate for an inner sense of direction to grow that stays with me. My friend Jonathon Porritt, in the memorial service for his father, said, "To be a child of such a man is to start out with as great a privilege as can be imagined – for which there can be no end of giving thanks." I too give thanks for mine. I shared with him not only a love of the sky but also a hunger for the land. This passion was consciously inside me from the age of ten, for I knew then that one day I would have land, and shape it.

The creek that runs through my secret spot is still partly frozen, leaving fossil remains of ice and crusts of snow from times gone by, of winters past. Wonderful to see little cascadings of water over rocks. Winter branches are still bare. Old white winter berries linger alongside pussy willows just appearing.

Even the pine trees, although they stay green, look a bit droopy in their winter hibernation. Icicles hang from the birch trees. As I look under the bank where some tree trunks have been hollowed, it's so inviting that if I were a coyote or a little mouse I would creep in and have a sleep. It must be a bit warmer under there. One leaf on a tree and one chickadee – almost the same colour. The rest bare branches. The leaves, the chickadee and the branches all grey, silver grey. A pine tree has fallen into the creek, and a second one on the other side, with a standing dead tree beside it. So we've got one, two, three logs that in time will float down the river.

Canada geese circle round with necessary talk, an outcry of where to nest. Their talk has the urgency that comes with seeking a site and hunting for food, a need that we don't have any longer. Little birds and squirrels create a whole different sound of chirping. Just the fun of it. No housing worries, no keeping warm worries.

Underfoot the squelch of frost just leaving the earth. There is a yield to one's footfall which is new since mid-February, when I was last here, and an anticipation as energy rises from the earth. Gone is the hush, gone is the numinous quality. I feel just happiness, rain, light and many new sounds, air abounding with the whirr of wings, busy nest-building.

All around is a-flutter with soft grey birds creating silver threads through the air, alighting on branches as if they are part of a design. They come closer and closer so as to see us better, encircling Bucky and me. I hear the whirr of wings behind us and above us, and we do not stir. The squirrels know this warm winter day is no time for hibernation. Out they come, leaping about on the higher branches, while the birds seek the lower ones, which reach out furthest, so that they can edge closer to have a better look at us.

It is worth the ordeal of living through an arduous winter to feel the special crispness and freshness in the air that you never get in a softer climate. Wind purrs softly (not always). Two old diamond willow bushes have clusters of branches blown by the wind, causing them to rest on top of each other, linking them together, creating an arch or a gate in nature. An arch in the wild designed by God. Without a doubt the most beautiful gateway I have seen in my life.

I lean against it for energy. Bucky on the other side of the water, with his body going in and out of the brush, and my hair going in and out of the branches; the same energy that is inside the willow is inside me now.

Bucky is pointing. I bend down beside him to see what he is about in the midst of startling light and shade patterns. He spots a wild grouse. I see white bird splatters on the barren ground. White is so dominant in the about-to-Spring earth. Shadowy patches on tree trunks; the light pitched at such an angle through the pine woods that the trees are reflecting on themselves, the lacery of a twig or the shadow of a branch revealed on the tree's own trunk.

Bucky's reservoir of limitless urine marks the world about him; his nose running close to the ground receives the past and present markings from others of his four-footed kind.

Where I'm sitting is quite moist, it's deep in the woods and there is no wind. I've just pulled on a sapling for support to climb an embankment and it came right up in my hand, because it wasn't rooted, and I realise how much to be cherished roots are. When you see them exposed from these pine trees along the river it's wonderful, because that's where all the little homes, caves, are made, and they are very inviting. Rootedness is just as important for human beings as it is for trees, for without it there can be no crown. When people have this sense of commitment to their country, a whole different being arises. Why else do animals give birth on the same ley line? Why else do people hark back to their natal spot as they get older – and very often return there?

Bucky goes quietly, yet is the biggest stirrer-upper of activity you can imagine. Right now I'm on the creek bank, and there's a chorus of coyotes caused by him. At first I thought he was in the middle of them, but no, he's with me, thank God. This coyote howling goes on and on, but luckily I've got him between my legs. His whole body is shivering, just anxious to get into it, I suppose. I guess one cannot take a walk with Bucky without expecting he will sniff round dens he shouldn't. Now they have come into my secret spot. I don't like to, but I'm tugging at Bucky's collar for him to leave this great scene. He doesn't want to leave these sounds, and after a few trots forward has a gaze back – he might just miss a little ripple of coyote activity. But their cries conceal danger, for a pack of coyotes is known to lure dogs into ambush.

Later I sit on the step and have before me a beautiful round, full, apricot moon, at mid-tree level. As a child I used to feel the moon followed me, and this is true tonight. There's one guiding star, one gentle little star. Water murmuring on my right, ancient frog sounds on my left. A few horses' feet, little snortings as they talk to each other, and a cow, the quiet call of a cow before we all go into dreamland. I wouldn't give up this moment for anybody or anything.

The Sacred and the Profane

In plains and woods where once did roam
The Indian and the Scout
The Swede with alcoholic breath
Sets rows of cabbages out.
(Old nursery rhyme)

The original wilderness of Alberta contained not only plants, trees and animals, but also people and their shelters.

Where I live now was once an Indian encampment. Looking down with an historic eye, I see teepees arranged in a circle and medicine wheels pointing north, south, east and west to spread their influence over the whole world. Looking down in the present, I see square houses, each one an islet unto itself, detached from its neighbours and from the outside.

Some people came from Europe to better themselves, some came to have a freer life with nature. One has to think of the Native who had been here for thousands of years, who had accustomed his body and mind, and truly listened, to the land whereon he felt blessed to dwell.

I have given you word portraits of two Hebrews, my father and my grandfather, and now I write of a Native. You, the reader, may wonder why. Well, there was a theory that the First People of our land were the lost tribes of Israel.

After the Spanish conquest of America, the word spread of the aboriginal Hebrew presence in the New World. Friar Torquemada, writing in Seville in 1615, warily referred to an unsigned manuscript which he felt was that of Friar Bartolomé de las Casas, the man who formulated the Indian-Israel theory. He saw a link. Not only did these people look alike; they also divided themselves into tribes, practised circumcision, marriage, divorce, polygamy, and so on. He put forward the theory that the tribes of Israel, uprooted by the Assyrians in 722 B.C., wandered through Asia, walked across the Bering Straits and became the first inhabitants on the American continent and forefathers of the Indians.

Who is to say? But with Chief John Snow of our province I at once felt an ease of access. He and other Chiefs had a quick way of entering into my essence. Perhaps we share a blood line – the link is suggested in Chief John Snow's *These Mountains are our Sacred Places,* in which he puts into words not only the reverence of his people for the land which was their birthright, but also his own respect for the God of the Hebrews.

"The Great Spirit, the Creator, in his wisdom has given to each climate its unique plant life and its unique animal life and its men and women, and He has given them a religion which is fitting to their needs. For the Hebrews who lived in the arid lands in the Middle East, with the thorny bushes and the cool, green grass near the wells and waterholes for the sheep and camels, He gave a religion to suit their way of life. For the people of this Great Island, with the shining mountains, the pine-covered hills, the grassy plains, the flowing streams, and the fish-filled lakes, He made a home for the moose and the buffalo and deer and taught His red children to pray as was suited to them.

"Our religion, the religion of this Great Island, is not contradictory to the teaching of the great Rabbis of the Hebrews, nor is it in conflict with the great Christian teachers…our religion professes faith in one Creator and acknowledges the unity and harmony of the whole environment – land, animals, birds, plant life, and men.

"As I look across the beautiful valley, it seems as if I am looking across the next one hundred years. I am reassured about the future… and I am reminded of the words of the Hebrew prophet of old, and I repeat:

They that wait upon the Great Spirit shall renew their strength,
They shall mount up with wings as eagles,
They shall run and not be weary,
They shall walk and not faint. (Isaiah 40:31)

"The old path is a proven path to travel on… It is the path of the Great Spirit, the Creator."

Over the centuries the Native people learned to live in harmony with the harsh climate. The European, reading exaggerated government advertising brochures and coming with European farming ideas, met a continent and weather totally unknown to him, something that would not yield its secrets in one or two years.

The Natives did no hay-making. The white man, with his tradition of haying in his land of origin, and finding here only a ninety-day growing season, caused everyone to run on the double through the time of haying. Because of the short summers, the new settlers had little time for worrying about their own dwellings or for celebrating nature as the native Indians did with their sun dances and pow-wows. The white man's pow-wow became a drunken letting off steam on a Saturday night.

Struggling with different soil, harsher climate, flies, bullflies, tent caterpillars, grasshoppers and drought was equivalent to the plagues of Egypt. Later came the bleak years of the Depression, which were so bad that there was a collusion of silence, so for many years no one knew, in the U.S.A. and Canada, how difficult it had been in the mid-Western region.

People struggling for existence under marginal conditions have neither time nor energy to feel consciously the contradiction between their actuality and their dream. Survival for them is a sufficient victory – and only those who truly heed how unforgiving their surroundings can be are able to come through. Perhaps this causes the sullen faces, muscled up like clenched fists, unwilling to let go of any tenderness or complicated emotion.

There is a legend of the ennobling wilderness and the wilderness man, as one found it with the true Indian Chief and some sensitive travellers to this land. The white man I talk of is cut off from his history and mythology, not in touch even with the implications of his landscape. Stampedes, rodeos and "pioneer days" have become big commercial operations. Skills once derived from the need for cattle-control on a working ranch are now sometimes circus events for prize money won by participants who follow the rodeo circuit, never setting foot on ranch land.

Nevertheless, many white people came with the same deep values as the Natives, who knew how to look for their religion and their heritage in the Old Man's Garden.

The wisest whom it was ever my fortune to meet was Milt Ward. Living to be a very old man, to the end of his life he had the understanding, as does the Native, to want to leave the land better for his sons than he found it. He taught me about the thickness of coat of an animal, and how to buy a good bull. I could never understand after that how men bought thin-coated breeds in our climate. He knew that before he put seed into the earth the plant formation would depend upon the quality of the soil, and that before the calf was born its bones and teeth were formed. He also gave me a healthy understanding of the early encounters of the ranchers and the oil men. When I talked to him on his 101st birthday, he was pure passion still about injustice; all age fell away. He died at 102.

Bob Blair, who formed Nova Oil Company, has the same sensitivity toward the land and its people, and he was the first oil boss to hire Natives. He works a lot from intuition, and this led to an easier interweaving. The Indians honoured him by making him Chief Iron Horse. It was wonderful to see him, in his oil concourse, splendid in Indian headdress and beaded waistcoat, dancing Indian dances in a circle. He gave a short talk, first in Blackfoot and then in English, saying, "That's the right way around, isn't it?"

The Alberta men who have understood and lived by the quintessence of good earth values are both dreamers and organisers, but they also make it possible for other people's dreams to happen.

These mountains are our temples, our sanctuaries, and our resting place.
They are a place of hope, a place of vision, a place of refuge,
a very special and holy place where the great spirit speaks with us…
These mountains are our sacred places. Chief John Snow

Speckles of snow are falling, not flakes, just little specks, and on Bucky's back too. Nobody's out this morning; it's just a slight regression into winter. Bucky doesn't have any squirrels or birds to link up with, so he has come back to sit with me. It's a silent morning, grey; it's wonderful to sit here and be snowed on, like baptism, as if Bucky and the trees and I are all being baptised, and greeted and blessed.

This is a great morning, too, for Bucky's game with sticks. He has this play in which he gets big branches and tramples around with them. Today he started like that, and now after a moment of stillness, with no animals to play with, he is again making his own fun, finding such a long stick that I have to make sure he doesn't brush me with it as he goes round me in circles.

Tree-sit. A walk. Bucky's faeces that he is so proud of, and a skeleton of a cow's head, the teeth upside down with the snow in its cavity. Ah, finally a squirrel chattering. A late rise this morning. Can you envision tall pussy willow bushes, their branches with soft buds being snowed on quietly?

It is clear that I was born for a placid country life. Placid it certainly is, so much so that the days are sometimes far more like a dream than anything real, quiet days of reading and thinking, watching the changing lights and the growing and fading of the flowers. The fresh, quiet days when life is so full of zest that you cannot stop yourself from singing because you are so happy. Many mornings I go to my secret spot with Bucky and say, "Aren't we lucky, Bucky! Aren't we lucky!"

Once in a while a man ought to focus his mind upon the remembered earth, giving himself up to a landscape he loves, or the landscape of his mind, and be in touch with it, with his hands, with his feet, with his being, over various seasons.

As I stand in stillness I think of my friend Alan McGlashan's words in The Climate of Delight: "Delight is a secret. And the secret is this; to grow quiet and listen; to stop thinking, stop moving, almost to stop breathing; to create an inner stillness in which, like mice in a deserted house, capacities and awarenesses too wayward and too fugitive for everyday use may delicately emerge. Oh welcome them home! For these are the long-lost children of the human mind. Give them close and loving attention, for they are weakened by centuries of neglect. In return they will open your eyes to a new world within the known world, they will take your hand, as children do, and bring you where life is always nascent, day always dawning. Suddenly and miraculously, as you walk home in the dark, you are aware of the insubstantial shimmering essence that lies within appearances; the air is filled with expectancy, alive with meaning; the stranger, gliding by in the lamplit street, carries silently past you in the night the whole mystery of his life...

"Delight springs from this awareness of the translucent quality in all things, whereby beauty as well as ugliness, joy as well as pain, men as well as women, life as well as death – the grinding clash of opposites between whose iron teeth all systems of philosophy are crushed at last to pulp – are seen to be symbols; in the true meaning of the symbol, whose Janus-face contains at once that which exists in time and space, and that which transcends it…

"Delight is a mystery. And the mystery is this: to plunge boldly into the brilliance and immediacy of living, at the same time as utterly surrendering to that which lies beyond space and time; to see life translucently."

Rumsey

"I wish they wouldn't talk about oil as if it was a faith. Anyone would think it was a church."
(Quoted by Anthony Sampson in *Company Man*)

When my father felt intimations of mortality before infirmities set in, he asked me, "If you were given money, what would you do with it?" To which I replied, "Give it back to you so that we could go together to buy land. All I want is land." And that is how I became the owner of Rumsey Ranch, named after Rumsey, Alberta, where the family homesteaded.

In taking upon myself the trusteeship of that ranch, I felt my Promised Land had become realised, envisioning that I would ride a horse and sit under a tree with none to disturb my dreams, that I would bring to my ranch the best of learning and culture.

Ancient man regarded himself as part of the world of nature and identified himself with the traits and powers of the more impressive creatures among his surrounding animal neighbours. Lewis Mumford stated his belief that people who live in concrete boxes, work in concrete factories, eat cornflakes for breakfast, allow the TV to do their dreaming for them, would perhaps go mad were it not that in their unconscious there still linger irrational layers of primitive jungle wildness. The interior animal asks to be accepted and permitted to live with us as a somewhat puzzling companion. Although always there, nevertheless it knows better than our conscious personalities, if we could only learn to listen to its dimly audible voice.

A more harmonious and integrated life comes from the fusion of conscious and unconscious, thus making possible a better stewardship of our own patch of earth, and enabling us to be a protector and guide to the humans and animals thereon.

I now come to the most difficult part of my story.

Living so close to the land I often peer into the sky for signs of weather – a chinook arch is always a blessing of warm weather. Some sunset skies are a shepherd's delight and some skies at sunrise a shepherd's warning, while we often repeat as children, "A wind from the east blows no good for man or beast". But at Rumsey, into my cherished landscape, into my home, it was a wind from the north which brought fumes from a gas Plant that were unnatural in colour, pinks and greens and putrid yellows.

In first coming to Rumsey, I had a deep wish to blend into the landscape, to find out about local ways, knowing that my neighbours and the Natives would understand more about survival than I did. As part of my purpose in creating a ranch life in Alberta, I was going to live in the wilderness: what I found was myself entangled with the wilderness of life in the oil companies.

The untouched and untilled field is more than a patch of earth; it is the body of the Earth Mother. The ability of the oil companies to divide this Earth Mother into a series of basement floors targeted for their exploitation came as a shock to me. In 1972 the Land and Forestry Department was put under the Department of Energy, and so it remained for twenty years. Alberta became known as the Texas of the North, as the government followed its policy of fast extraction, and the chief criterion was that of making fast money. I learned that I only possessed Surface Rights, which meant that just the surface portion of the earth's crust was mine to love and tend; below that was an industrial quarry to be freely excavated by competing companies. Smaller oil companies had the right to explore only 200, 300 or 400 feet deep, but the big boys had drilling rights down to 1,500 and 2,500 feet, and even beyond to any depth. I know how vital industry is in our lives, and of course I wanted to work with them, hoping for a seismic shift on their part.

The seeming blunder of buying land that had a gas well in its midst (thinking it was an industrial plant like any other) was perhaps not chance, for the drilling into the surface and sub-surface of my land produced unsuspected springs in myself. As the odours and fumes were not going away, and as I did not wish to go away, I set about making bureaucratic tracks in the hope of repairing the damage done to the earth. This led me into the world of industry, law and finance. These tracks took twenty years of my life.

My father never believed in fussing a situation. He would say, "If someone displeases, be it a doctor or a lawyer, pay your bill and go away. The truth will out." I didn't have patience to wait for the truth to manifest itself in regard to the arrogance of the oil companies drilling under my land at that time and, being intoxicated with the notion that justice is for everyone, I sought to put things right. It was here that I parted both with my father's ways and with the usual norms of behaviour in such situations.

On my nocturnal walks, with the soughing of the wind in the pinewoods, I pondered on the coil of things in my life; I wanted to try to think out these awful days which were so unlike any other.

Not only were the chemicals from the gas Plant poisoning my enzyme system, so that my body was unable to do the complex things it was designed to do, but I felt that a weight had been dropped on my heart, pressing down on it and making it difficult to breathe. When a man dies there is a proper burial; when part of the earth, or a body of water dies there is no funeral, just an uneasy turning away.

It is strange to walk at night and listen to the dwindling sound of one's own footfalls, but this is what I was doing, and as I did so a clarity of feeling came to me. I knew I could not run from the situation; I could not be permitted to turn my back on this evil. Something that seems disgusting still shares the truth of its being with everything else. I must approach this reality, endure, and hopefully proceed; I must meet it, and "them", face to face. So this struggle with the oil companies opened a destiny, the dying of the old me and the slow birth of a new.

In the 1970s the world was afraid to offend the Arab countries, and by the same token the people of Alberta did not wish to upset the oil companies. The usual procedure was that a farmer whose land had been invaded by pipelines would protest, would be awarded an amount based on land value and would then go away, leaving the oil company to continue exactly as it pleased.

So when Canadian Broadcasting Corporation's 6 o'clock news blazed the item, "Miss Hanan goes to war with Big Oil", my family were chagrined at the idiocy of such a posture. A then good friend, the chief geologist at another major oil company, wrote to say that if I was really determined to go ahead and fight the oil companies I should never cross his threshold again. My best friend, married to a lawyer, decided they should cease their association with this embarrassment, and most of my hired hands became nervous of their connection with me. No one with any sense, it was said in bewilderment, would even dream of issuing an injunction on an oil company. I just believed that we are all children under the same sky and that conciliation would for me be a crime against humanity.

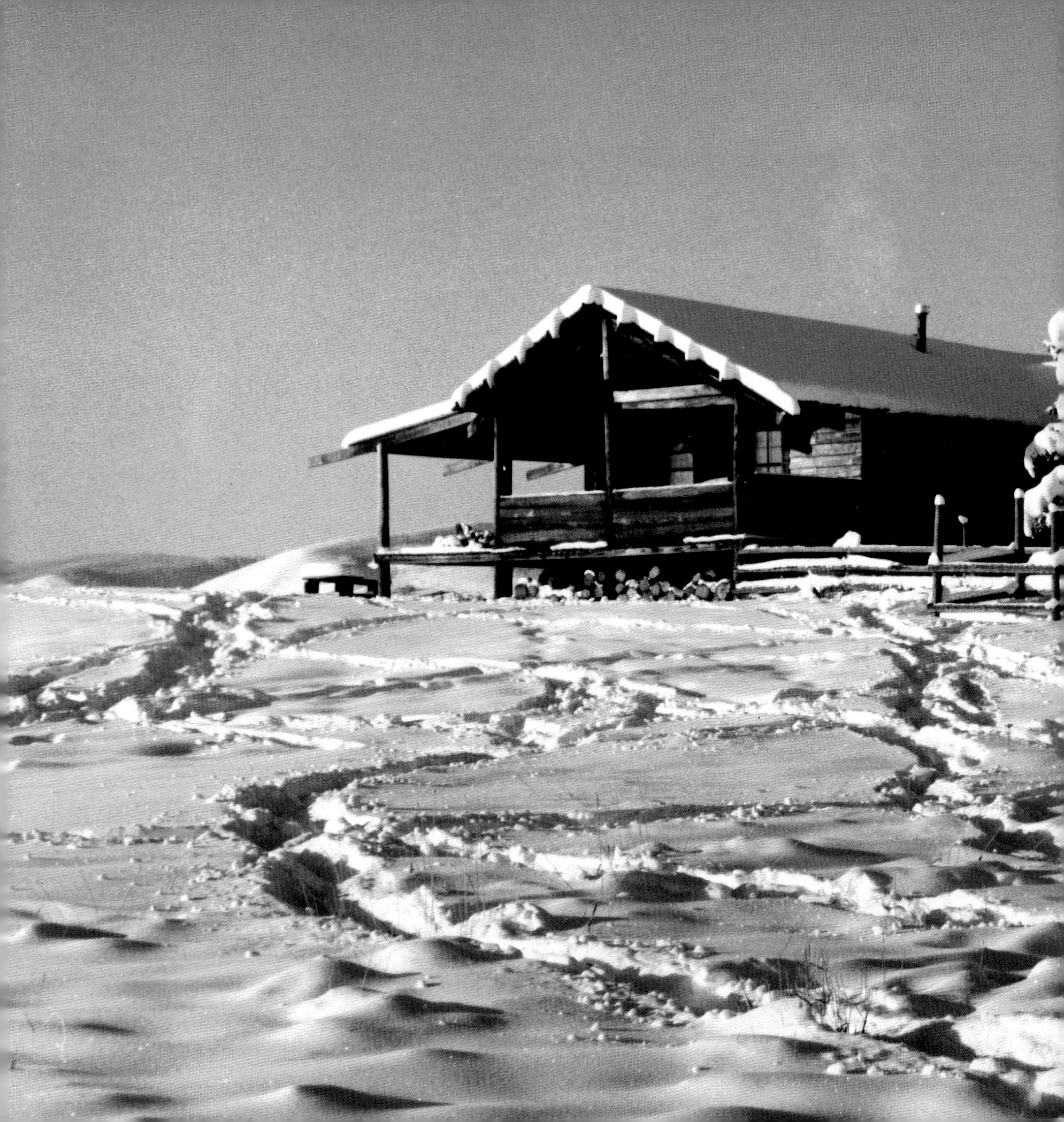

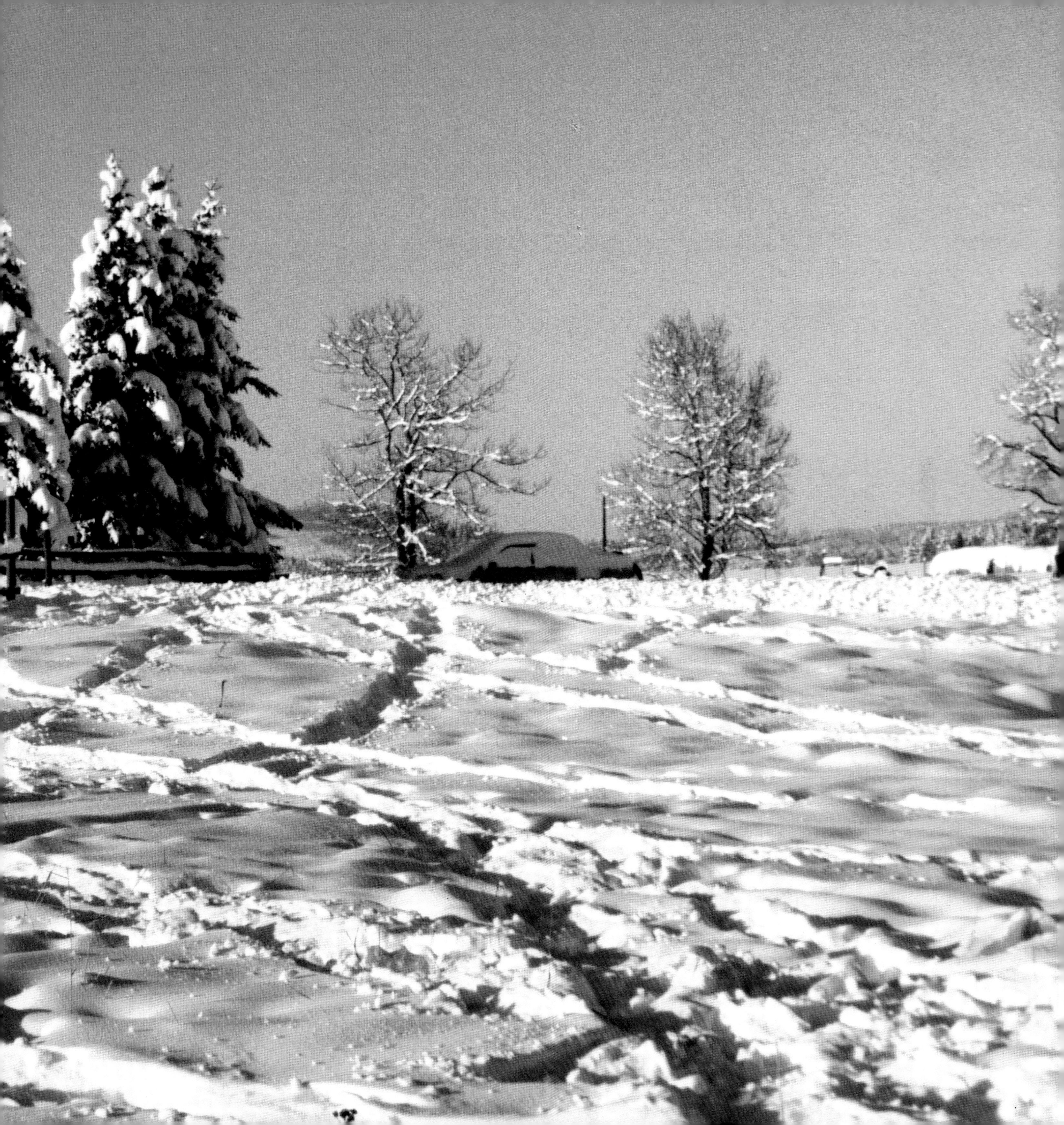

Poison enters one's land and one's being. It was very hard, however, in the sealed glass cages of most of Calgary's offices, to make people feel the insidious fumes spewed out by the Plant and understand how deeply they invaded one's very being, so denial of any harm set in. As with the nuclear energy situation at Hadfield, Oregon, and the unfortunates there "down-wind" of the plant who suffered for generations, here too with neurotoxins in the scrubbing agents I had the same denials, and heard as they did, "It is good for you". How do the "down-winders" convey to those who have windows that do not open what it is like to have their pollutants invade one's being?

Twenty years of meetings with men at the top in government and industry have given me a new insight into the world where the market place captures the souls of those who single-mindedly follow this path. These men are trapped by their fear and greed, and in return they use fear and greed to control others. Dedication to efficiency at all costs is total, the attitude being, "You come to meetings unless you're dead, and if you don't come you *are* dead". The arrogance of such people is amazing – it amused me to hear one man say in all seriousness, "Rome wasn't built in a day because an oil company didn't have the contract".

Even they were humbled, though, when they tried to harness a ship to an iceberg, hoping it would carry them where they wanted to go. But in the vast frozen land of the North man and his technological toys have little place: drift ice, calving icebergs and avalanches of ice that come straight from the glaciers take no account of his ambitions. So the "berg" which they imagined would tow their ship took a different course and broke up. The ship, with its costly rig, dropped away with the current and the tide below. This world was so foreign to me that I was able to view it with detached wonder.

Industrial time to me seems to go in fits and starts and self-imposed deadlines. There was perpetual change amongst the oil company's people, and I have watched whole generations of personnel succeed one another in breathless haste. But I could see the world would not fall apart if they could not drill whatever, whenever.

When I began to deal with the oil companies, I started to feel something was amiss: in a democracy one should be able to speak one's mind freely about the preservation and health of the land. I decided to approach the government boards, all until then unknown to me. In the early seventies the Energy Resources Conservation Board did not take me seriously; they called me "dearie", patronised me, and thought me quite funny.

I write of the flowing of two currents. The Old World industry, and Big Oil within it, is one: I am part of the other wave rising. Small are the number who see the world with their own eyes and feel with their own hearts that there is now irresistibly growing round the globe a stirring of hearts which will not be overridden by juggernauts. One can relate to a symbol or the logo of a company, or to hidden forces within each one of us: I chose the latter path, and in doing so I have met some great men in industry, law and banking.

One of the honest voices was Walter Trost's, so I circumnavigated every board and everyone else and simply talked to him. Walter was a Rhodes scholar who went on to become Dean of Graduate Studies at Dalhousie University, and then Vice-President of the University of Calgary and head of the Environment Conservation Authority. The terms of reference of the ECA were to look at all sides of the conservation issue with complete objectivity, and Walter Trost was well equipped to hold this position. Natives and white men alike respected the hearings that he held, for he truly cared and truly listened. He was asked to write on the effects of sulphur emissions from oil wells on land, animals and people. The report was a model of good writing and honesty, way beyond the level of most government documents.

He too knew the nightmarish qualities of sour gas, while everyone else in the government at that time was trying to do an "Emperor's clothes" act, and the oil companies were the judge, the jury, the trial and all; for they did their own readings of their own emissions. (The government could not afford to do it, they said.) Had it not been for Walter, I should not have been able to weave a path through this web of misinformation.

Sadly, Walter Trost died in the autumn of 1993. I still, to this day, feel uplifted to remember him, and the joy of listening to his beautiful mind expound on various subjects. He is one of my people treats, and one of life's blessings.

With the tide of public opinion running so strongly against me, it was difficult to engage either a lawyer (because they were afraid that accepting my brief could lose them lucrative work from the oil companies in future) or an engineer, but with both I was lucky. Frank Burnet studied at Queen's before going on to practise law in Alberta. He was a fisherman scholar; he had about five Hardy rods in his room, and he believed deeply in fly-fishing. He approached fishing with the same kind of philosophy and scholarship that he brought to the law.

Having an awareness of the seasonal cycles, he taught me about the cycles in financial trends; at the height of the boom he made me face the imminent slump. Along with the cowboy, he taught me the importance of waiting for the right moment.

Mr Burnet and I shared a background in classics. He was big enough to tell me that I wrote a convincing letter, and that I should write direct to the oil companies rather than through a law firm. If I hired a lawyer, they would hire six, and the thing would be set into a frozen mould; but if he stayed in the background as a depot for letters and I was the one to go forward, much more could be accomplished. He enjoyed working with me and I with him; he said I never became so obsessed with the situation that I would be overwhelmed, whereas some farmers who had started battles previously had been.

I would sit in his office for two or three hours at a time, learning about Canadian history and the British North America Act. It was his knowledge of the oil and gas industry of Alberta, and of Alberta's politics and its legal connections, and his respect of me, that gave me support in what I was doing.

Success, to me, is epitomised by someone who can go through the four seasons of life and still have a very great lightness and a twinkle in the eye. All the time I was seeking counsel from Mr. Burnet, I did not realise I was talking to a man in his eighties. He worked at law every day of his life until he died at the age of ninety-two. His interest was always fresh; he simply worked fewer hours. His secretary, Cathy Porter, was with him from the time she was seventeen, through school, marriage, motherhood and grandmotherhood, until his death. I have never known a lengthier, more loyal working relationship.

Mr Burnet put me in the care of his partner, John Rooke, now Justice Rooke, who worked in great harmony not only with me but also with Ed Jones, my engineer. When he agreed to help me, Ed had had a heart attack and wasn't working; he was so frail that it was a great effort to walk more than a few steps, but as time went by he grew from strength to strength, and enjoyed the excitement of being part of putting things right. He had been involved in gas Plant engineering, and felt a justifiable anger towards the industry. His contribution was very great – not least in a splendid TV appearance which he made on my behalf.

Solzhenitzyn said that a society which is lawless, such as Russia was under the Communists, is not a society. But a society like the one we have in North America, spending millions looking for the technical, legal loopholes to escape doing the proper thing, no matter what the ethics, is not a society either. Law is not just a pathway to success, to a big house or a political job: it is a very important part of our society and should, therefore, be given deep respect.

Poison seeps into one's land and the living creatures thereon, man, animal and vegetable.

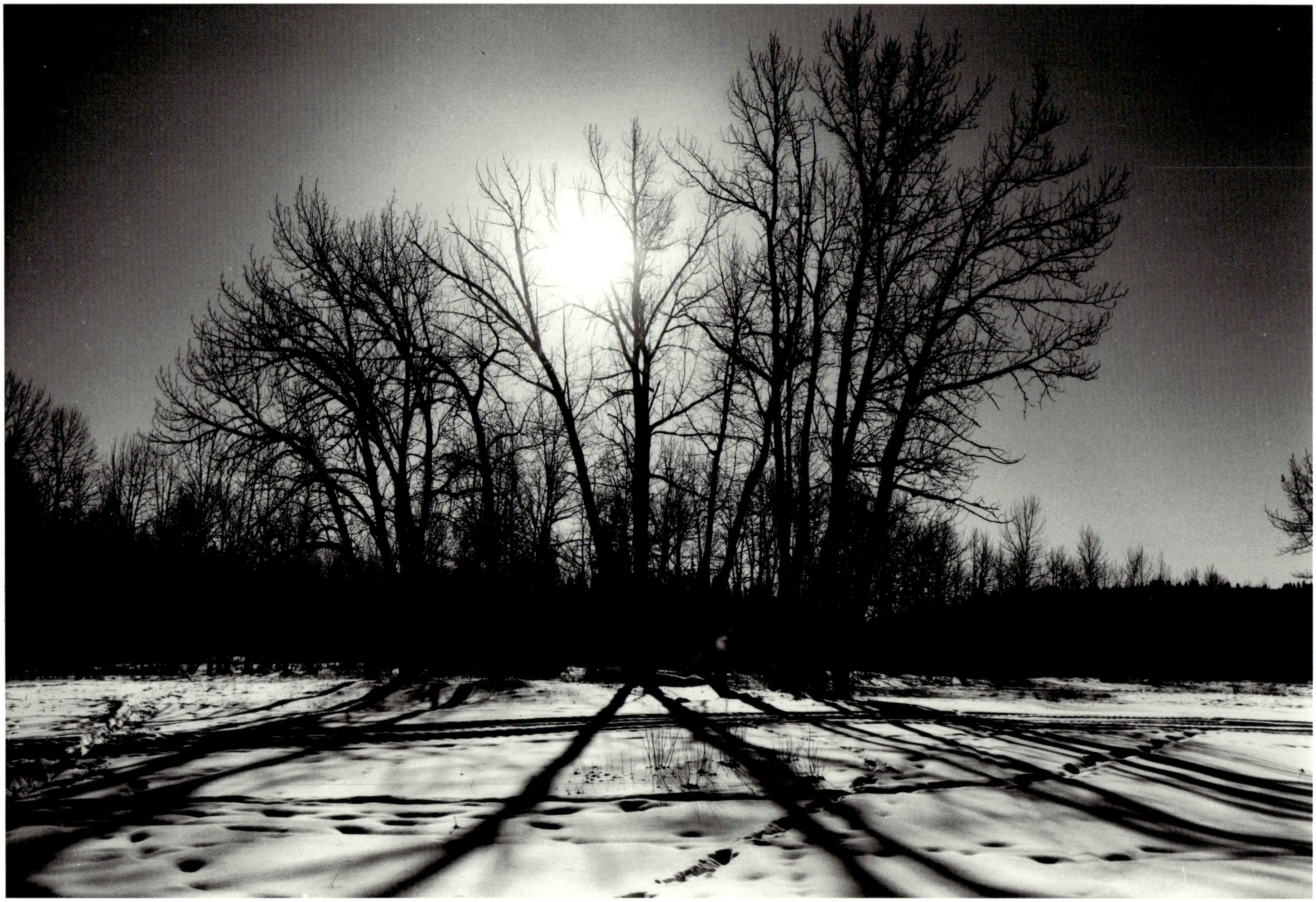

April's end, May's beginning. Snow melting, water running here and there. Heaven linking with earth, the rain from the heavens linking up with a body of water in my secret spot. "The Spirit of God was on the face of the waters." Have you ever noticed that as each raindrop strikes the water it forms a circle, so that there is a play of circle upon circle, forming and re-forming with each fresh raindrop?

Simone Weil writes, "Contemplation of the circular movements of intelligence in the heavens should serve as a guide for the circular translations of thought in ourselves, which are related to them. But the heavenly movements are untroubled while ours are disturbed; we should be instructed by this and take part in the essential rectitude of heavenly proportions. By the imitation of God's circular motions, which are absolutely without error, we should make our own errant motions stable."

Another day, looking at a backwater on the way to my secret spot, I saw a water spider; each time it moved it created a circle. "Everything the power of the world does is done in circles…The wind, in its greatest powers, whirls…Birds make their nests in circles, for theirs is the same religion as ours…Even the seasons form a great circle in their changing, and always come back again to where they were." (Chief Black Elk, Ogalala Sioux).

We have to bring the cyclical motion of the day and the seasons into life, for otherwise we create physical and psychic imbalance where we should find amplitude of resonance in our beings.

The squirrels chatter intensely, for I have been away for three weeks, and they are naïve enough to feel that this is their world exclusively. As I walk to the tree gate that takes me away from their domain, the chattering subsides and I know they feel relieved. I see entry holes to little squirrel homes in the womb of the earth, and a cache of pine cones gathered together in the upper courtyard of Squirrel City.

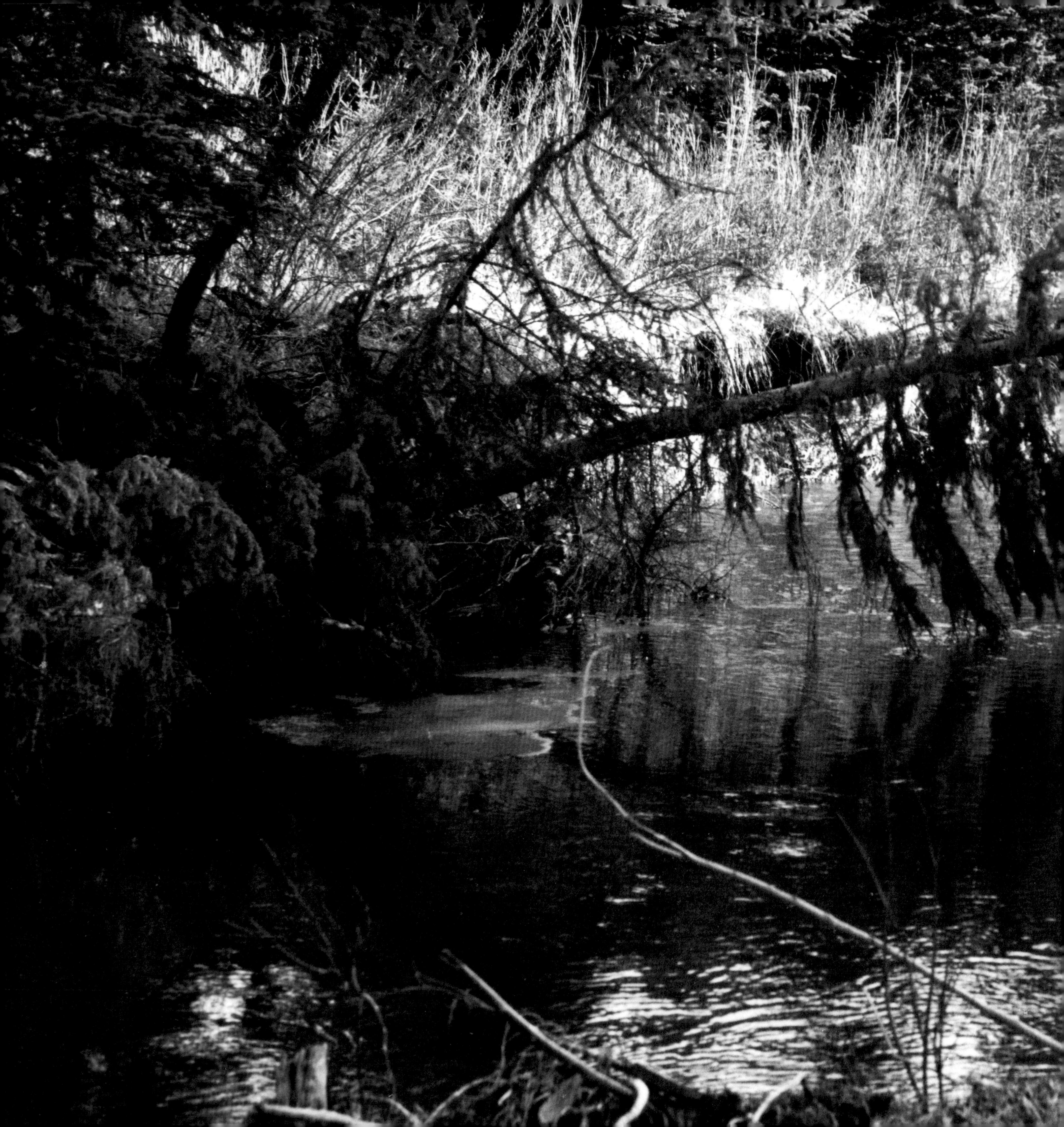

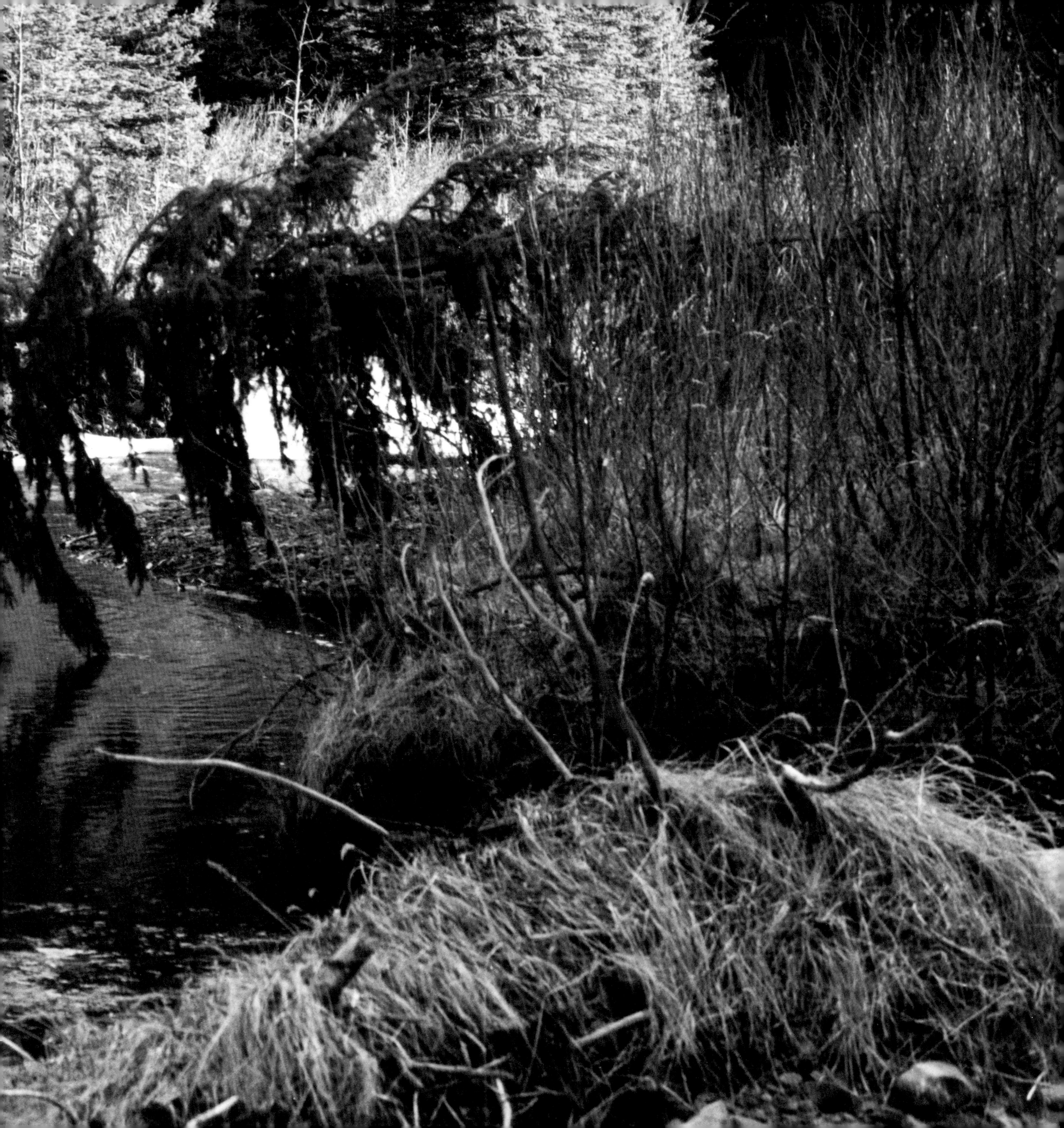

Birds flying in, of every wing, so that, as I walk by each little backwater and pond, touching down on the water are ducks and geese. Some pools are so special I daren't go near for fear of disturbing their privacy of nesting.

I love anything that comes from the sky, snow in Canada and rain in Scotland. It is wonderful to have the geese out there, to have the geese nesting beside us. Two pairs came up the creek, and then went off for the morning. Gone is the silence. Sounds abound – geese, frogs, creek rushing. Let's look for a minute; let's go very slowly, and listen to all the new sounds that are about – birds making nests, a cuckoo, a pileated woodpecker burrowing holes with his beak into the trunk of a tree. Those birds have been far south over the winter, and one can hardly imagine what they have endured, making their way back here. Some will nest here, but others will fly on to the Arctic.

All these things are just samples of something greater, but they convey what I know is true – that I would not have been able to follow the compass of my own being, as nature had predisposed me, if it had not been for the earth of my native country, the land, that vast land and immense sky, and all the manifestations of nature and life upon it.

I am going to stretch out fully and receive the morning sun in the midst of this private, God-made grove that has survived the invasion of the oil company and whatever they have done. Mindless of the small scale of the creek, they took it as a source for their big Plant. The creek dried up in that section, but lo and behold a little backwater was created that fed the roots and allowed this grove to survive. The trees have taken twenty years to recover from the shock; they stood, barely ticking over, some standing dead, but now they look as if they are coming back to life. To observe this first regeneration is marvellous.

With the snow moving away, the push of plants can be seen. And with the thaw in the ground, Bucky begins to paw the earth here and there. There's nothing more frenzied and revelling than Bucky pawing the earth, then sniffing it, then pawing further, and then sniffing further. Most often he comes up with nothing. Lately he has taken to travelling around with a deer calf's head and vertebrae dangling from his mouth as he runs about on one of our walks. There is no greater pride than in this trophy, shown to all as he trots along, jaws seized on a new-found object.

One night he presented me with a huge, bushy coyote tail, a pleasure I would have been happier without. I told him to drop it and come indoors. He wouldn't come near me the whole night long, and in the morning the first thing he did was to pick up the gift he had given me, which I had ungraciously rejected.

We went again to the woods to listen and watch, and they had never seemed so alive and fresh as they did this time. I have a special tree, and I like to sit with my back against it, thinking things out, watching the changes as the seasons pass, but today I thought to discover a new tree trunk, and found one with a lacery of twigs, with lichen and moss hanging from it. The lower branches were issuing forth like the ribs of a teepee, so I could sit in their shadow, and look down to the water stream without being seen.

But a short way from this experience I became dizzy with polluted air. To live with the immediacy of incredible beginnings – trees that have never been touched since man was here – and poison gas pervading them and you: this is what has happened at Rumsey Ranch; poignancy of poison in air and water. As the poet William Empson said, "Slowly the poison the bloodstream fills." Sometimes it is not so slowly.

God's silence. A curtain of silence through which one hears and feels everything is always interrupted here by the man-made noise of gas wells. In the landscape of the future, I hope industry will allow respect for a spot like this, and that what has happened here will not repeat itself elsewhere.

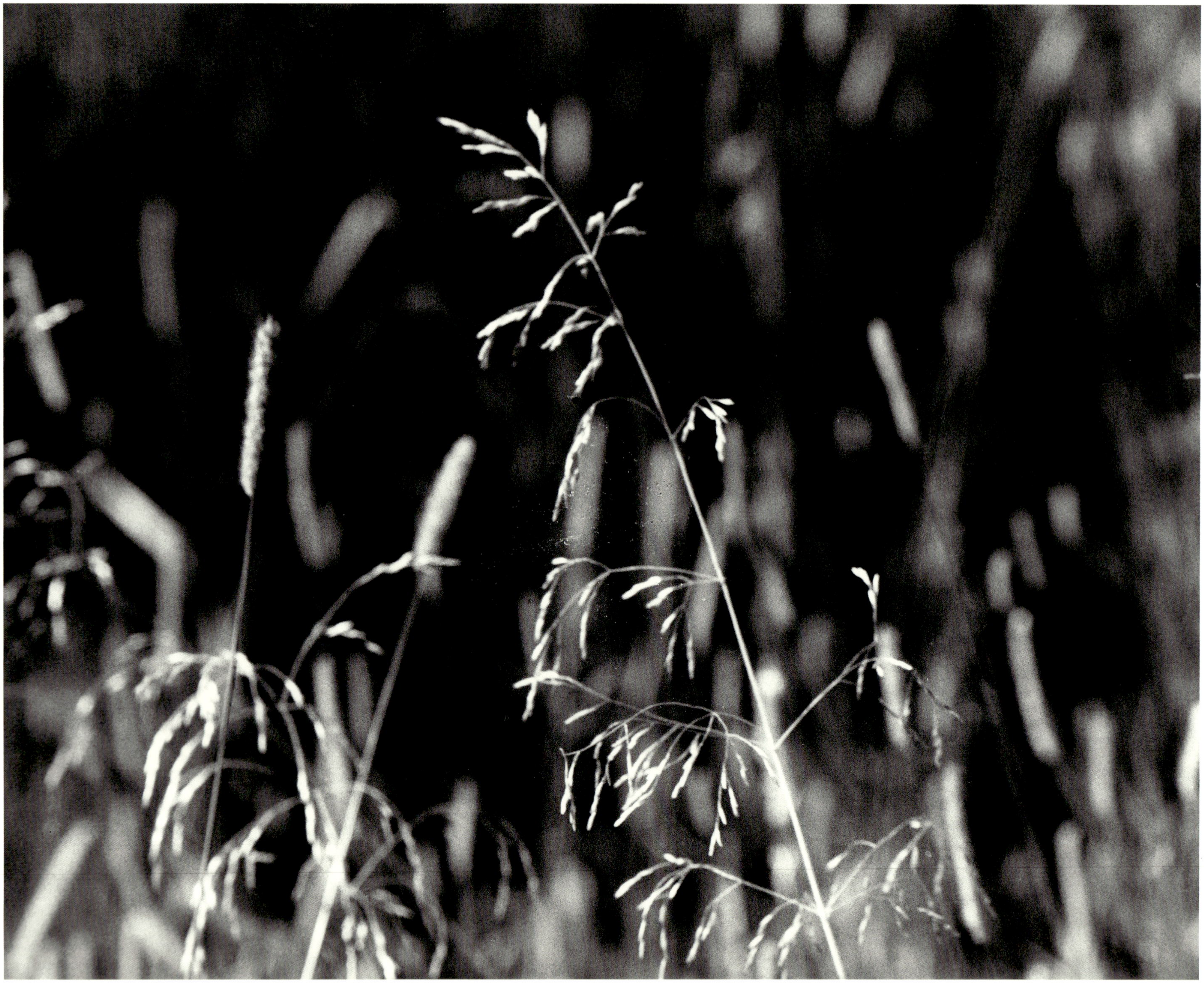

Meeting the Land

The range of the mountains is his pasture and he searcheth after every green thing.
Job xxxix, 8

As the Old Testament puts it so pithily, all flesh is grass. All animals, including the most determined of carnivores, eat plants, if not firsthand, then at second, third or fourth. The Inuit of the Arctic, who used to be known as the Eskimo, were reputed, before they took to softer southern ways, to have existed entirely on the flesh of seals and fish and to eat no vegetables whatever. Yet the seals eat fish, fish eat small fish, and they in turn eat smaller creatures such as tiny shrimps, which themselves graze on vast clouds of microscopic algae, floating in the surface waters of the oceans. Algae are plants. All flesh is indeed grass.
David Attenborough, *The Private Life of Plants.*

Part of ranching, and an important part, is management of all the wilderness, hillsides and plants, and the orchestration of the right number of cattle, so that they have enough luscious bites, as do the deer and elk who, in greater part, go near the cool mountain tops in the summer and return to the valleys in the winter.

When I came to Rumsey, I was appalled to find the grazing pastures chewed to billiard-ball smoothness by a herd of five hundred, so I thought it best to start with seventy-five cows, slowly to allow the range to come back, and build up the herd from there. Where is the economic sense in over-use? Where is the sense in a dust bowl? Without grass there is no ranch. I can see the tearing hurry because of the brief summer – but if the husbanding is not carried out in nature's time and way, the money windfall will be short-lived. Alex Johnston, a now-deceased authority on range management, has pointed out that since the white man arrived only half the variety of plants that had once flourished still survive.

Long before I came, everywhere on these steep slopes was the loveliest sprouting and spurting of seeds. The hills and hollows of these ranges were brimming with the sights and smells of plant life. Plants grew on every hill and under every green tree, losing their leaves, regaining them, and thereby becoming renewed. They re-enacted, for all who were here before me, the whole cosmos, revealing endless regeneration.

Strong native grass can stand tall longer when struck by storms; tame grass is more easily flattened.

In not wishing to over-graze, in leaving some of the plants so that they may have enough vigour to fight back, is manifest my anxiety not to exhaust the essence, the vivifying force of this vegetation. Rather do I perceive my purpose as that of allowing and even abetting the circuit of bio-cosmic energy, and particularly vegetative energy, on a vast scale.

An unspoiled landscape and an unspoiled way of life always draw me, but to make the ranch viable I need the many skills of genuine cowboys, who can turn their hand to anything, be it soldering a copper pipe for plumbing, mending a harness, or tending sick animals. On my part this requires an overview of all the components involved, for good management combines the big and the small. We pay for everything in life, and with the joys and the blessings comes the responsibility of keeping everything in gear.

Cowboys do not like doing much with tractors, but because of the smaller scale of my operation there is a need for a cowboy who can both ride a horse and get on the machines. With the responsibility of owning land one has to have the surveillance of the land – of grasses native and tame. The tame necessitate re-seeding about every five years with an appropriate mixture that will yield high protein quality but will be hardy enough to ensure that the root systems will not suffer from winter kill.

The machinery is required for land preparation to create a willing soil for the seed bed and for gathering the hay at harvest time. Because of being in the foothills at an altitude of four thousand feet, we have to get the seeds in and the crops out in ninety days, for there could be snow at each end of this period. Because of the long winter, we plan on feeding for six months.

There are four miles of fencing to attend to each spring before we put the cattle out on the grazing pastures. During the winter elk traverse the ranch, and when they jump over the wires they often loosen them. Also, during winter storms, trees may fall on to the fencing and create chaos, so we have to saw down the fallen trees and tighten the wires, leaving the bottom wire at a distance close enough to the ground for the calves not to slip underneath.

My domestic herd cannot roam as freely as the deer or the elk, for they are fenced in. Usually we move them by horseback, or by salt rotation, putting blocks of salt where we want some grazing done in newer pastures. Cows are rather inclined to linger in a meadow they like, but we do not want over-grazing going on into winter, as the plants must not be chewed to the ground. One must respect the whole community of plants, and once a cow selects a favourite and overeats, the competition of the others begins. We need to keep a good plant stem height so as to hold the snow, thus containing the moisture for a future year.

If the cow favours a certain herb to the exclusion of others, it may mean that one of the more aggressive remaining plants takes over in this vacuum and does not allow the favoured plant to come back the following year. I like to follow the method of Voisin, a French veterinarian. He wrote on natural grazing, and stressed the importance of leaving a good stem so that the plant has enough fight to grow back again. We are in long grass country – much of Alberta is short grass – but sometimes there are surprisingly more nutrients in the sturdy short grass than in the long.

One of the big early ranchers was Pat Burns, who used to say that so long as you hold on to the tail of the cow you'll be all right. A good stockman is a rich treasure with a total awareness of animal behaviour and the controlled tension of an athlete. A mutual trust evolves between himself and his herd. He knows that unless the cattle are happy he cannot be happy. Good herd management is just like good management of one's own life: it comes down to stress management. Cattle that are least stressed are going to do best; they are not going to lose weight, and their bodies are going to function properly. It is beautiful to see how tender and gentle the cowboy can be as he helps a cow to calve or a very weak calf to stand up and suck. It is a case of just the right amount of interference with nature.

So, along with the cow and horse and elk and deer roaming and eating at earth's table, there is now myself, collecting the annual herb harvest. Today I spot a drift of sage at the foot of trembling aspens, and gather some for winter soup. What I take part in is the man-plant circuit, that long, strong link between us and some kinds of vegetation as a continuous circulation of life between all creatures and plants. Herbs in history have cures for us all, for they embody within them this source of life.

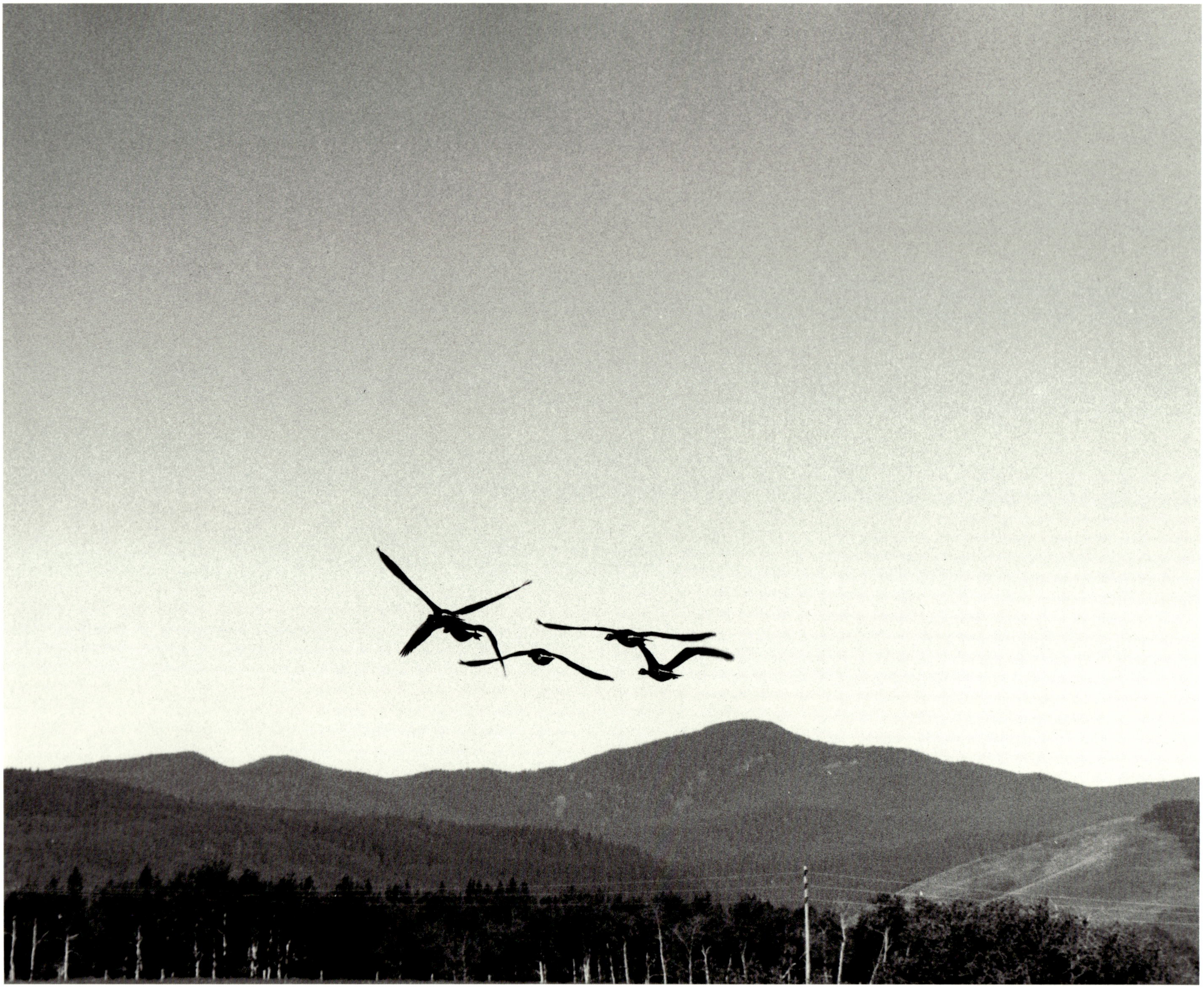

The whirr of wings and the murmur of water, these are the two main sounds of this spring. It is mid-May, and a marriage between snow and rain has coated every branch. The snow is sticky, like flour and water, and doesn't blow off. The sounds are different when it snows, almost an immediate hush of silence happens. Even the creek doesn't sound so vociferous in its running as it did yesterday. In the stream each little droplet of snow is met by the water.

On the route to my secret spot I nibble balsam poplar. My cat Willow has followed me, and she miaows very strongly in the background, for she wants me to come back. She sounds fearful, and listening to her I go to the source of her distress: a coyote den and black coyote manuring in its doorway. A coyote den almost under our window created in the root of a tree, out of sight, tucked under a creek bank ledge. Willow, God coming through her half-closed yellow eyes, shares with me something meaningful. Bucky dealt with this too nearby source of fear, the coyote den, in his own fashion; he crossed it with his pee-mark, signature tune.

Through tall balsam, hazel and willow, all just leafing out, I make my way. In the thickness of growth, tripping over branches underfoot, I guess this is our northern equivalent of jungle, but there are no machetes here. Cowboys do not like it, because it cannot be penetrated by men on horseback, just by four-footed wild life, Bucky and me.

Observing things from Bucky's eye level, I see a blade bone in the woods with a bit of greening on it, a mixture of vertebrae, earth, pinecones, and little pine needles from last year all together. A gully and a whole surface revolution of the root system just above it, an incredible network of roots and root hairs woven together to feed this trio of three pine trees.

At this hour, every tree has a shadow, one long tree trunk and one little shadow. The sun is rising in the east, not quite above the woodland, and casting its light on this wood in the west. It is so thick, but all around there is a corridor of light and shadow. I love the darkness in the centre of the woods and the light at the edges, and then the lovely reflections on this backwater. The nest-building sounds have a joy and gentleness about them, with none of the feverish activity the squirrels display for their winter houses.

Before me a tree soars up with a big root system and a whole spread of nibbled pine cones, the shells all interweaving with the roots, and tiny holes where the squirrels go in and out.

I see my first wild strawberry flower of this spring. The warmth has brought out not only the pine and poplar resin but also the fragrance of the leaf decay that has blanketed the earth, as well as bugs. Again, light and shadow, for until now one could keep doors and windows open, in the period between the deep freeze of winter and the gentle warmth of now, with no pest immigration.

Dandelions for breakfast, so life cannot be all that bad. Bucky and I alongside the water, drinking in pure heaven.

As I return from my secret spot the creek makes so much sound; it is a barrier insulating me from linear time. As I pass, the branches drop little showers of snow on me, and spray me with more little showers as they spring back. Sometimes they slap me in the face too. I don't mind when they brush along my jacket, but a slap in the face hurts.

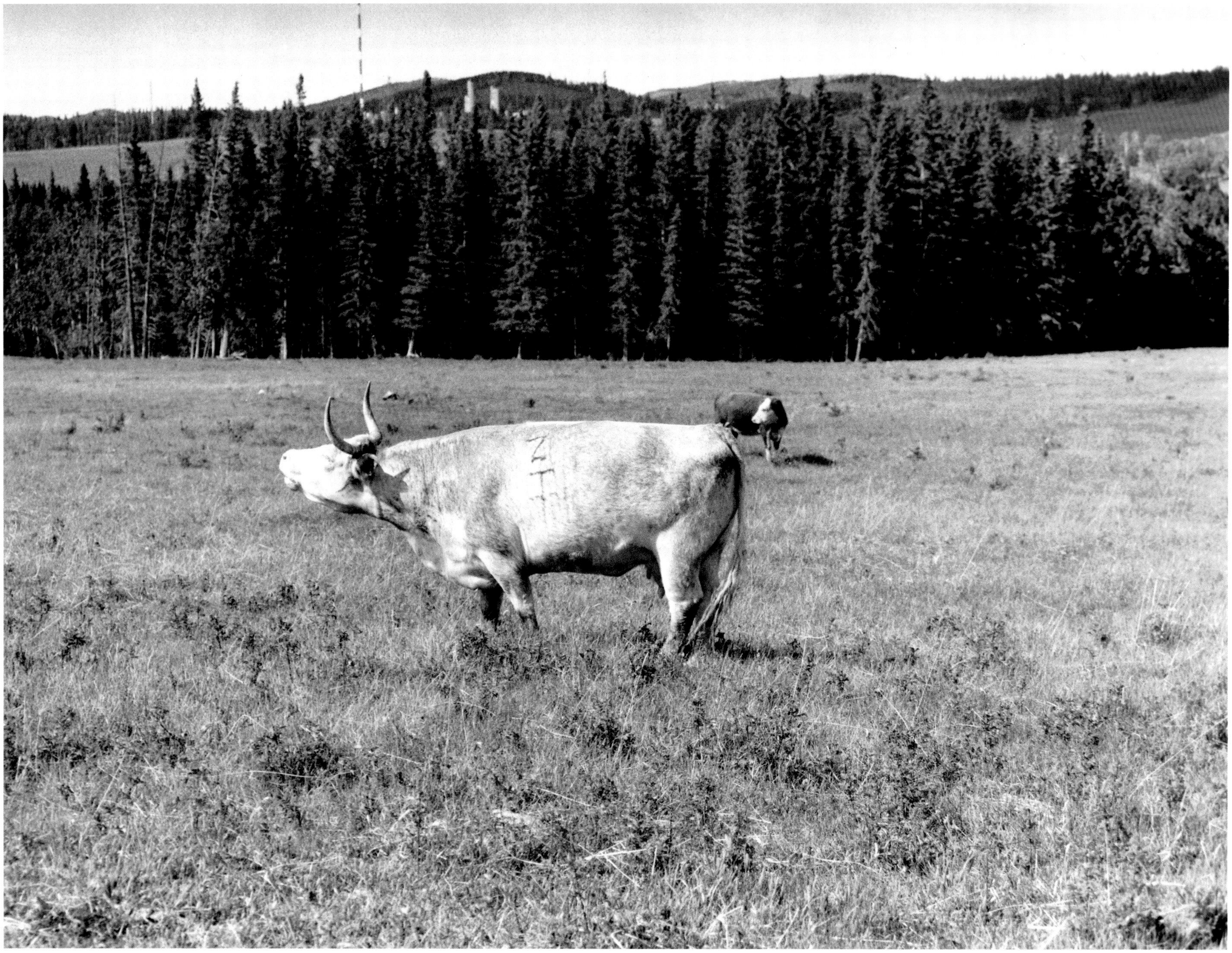

Jim Commodore

"Still Followin' that Ol' Cow"

Dealing with men, I usually ask them if they have any trouble working for a woman. I say at the beginning, "If you and I are big enough, when we're wrong, to admit that we're all fallible, we shall never have to justify ourselves to each other, and then we shall have something strong." Basically, my philosophy is to develop trust so that we never do have to justify ourselves. I feel that when men are strong and sure of themselves, there is no discomfiture in working for a woman.

There is no point in getting into a bull-rutting situation: it wouldn't be useful. It might do for a man working for another man – they would have a big roar and bellow and then it would be over – but this wouldn't do for a woman. I seek someone with similar values about the soil and a liking for the same breed of cow.

Tolstoy opens *Anna Karenina* with the sentence, "All happy families are more or less like one another; every unhappy family is unhappy in its own particular way." This is true, too, of cowboys: the "good" ones share a respect for humans and animals, for the law which cherishes them and which they in turn cherish; the "bad" ones are bad in different ways, but two things they lack – reverence and humility. They are at war both with themselves and with the world they live in.

So, with this in mind, I advertised in *The Western Producer*: "Cow-calf operation 250 cows, 40 miles from Calgary, wishes all-round ranch hand, experienced with modern machinery. Excellent housing facilities. Salary to be discussed. Permanent employment for suitable man. If married important that wife does not dislike ranch isolation."

To which James Wilfred Commodore replied:

"In regards to your ad. for a ranch hand in the Western Producer, I am very interested in locating in the Calgary area.
I am 36 years old, married with no children, and am presently employed looking after a herd of 800 head of cattle of which some 625 are mature she stuff. I have held this position for the past six years.
I was raised with livestock and have worked with them since leaving school. I am well acquainted with most diseases and treatments as well as calving problems and how to handle them. I'm also a graduate of Graham's School for Cattlemen of Garnet, Kansas. Have done a bit of welding and am familiar with most types of haying equipment.
You mention ranch isolation which is an attraction as my wife and I both enjoy working and living in a more remote and peaceful location.
If an interview is required we could meet with you at your convenience.
J.W.Commodore"

When I phoned for a recommendation from the MacIntyre Ranch, where he had worked before, I was told that he was the best stockman in Alberta. That he read a cow well, that many cowboys liked working with their legs dangling (sitting in the saddle), but Jim was not one of those, he would fix fences or machinery and turn his hand to anything.

Jim came to work for me, and what followed is one of my life's treats.

To talk of Jim it is as important to tell of his father, Wilfred Commodore, known as Curly Commodore. Curly was surely part-Indian, and he worked for the Prairie Farm Rehabilitation Association (a government agency for the rehabilitation of prairie pasture) in Saskatchewan. He is dead now, but each year when the PFRA meet they hold a one-minute silence for him. This honour, bestowed on a man by people who are harsh judges of others, bespeaks the character of that man.

Snowed in from Christmas until Easter, visitors to their home were a rarity. Wintry solitude and silence were a part of the rhythm of their lives, and a rich harvest of wisdom emanated therefrom. Jim's uncle said of him as a child that he was a very fine boy, but the trouble was that he always had everything figured out. He (Jim) spent a lot of time watching and judging and figuring it all out.

Jim once told me that if anyone came to work for his father or for him and asked what was needed to be done, they would be sent away. His father had taught him that you don't need a guy who has to ask what needs to be done. There is a photograph of Jim, aged two, standing in his father's cowboy boots with his father's hat falling over his head and carrying a small rope in his hands. He showed me this photograph, observing, "The making of a cowboy, you have to start at two". He believed that if you started later you might learn how to move a cow, but you would not learn how to think like a cow.

At the age of nine his father sent him up a windmill that did not work. When Jim descended and admitted that he had not fixed the windmill, his father answered, "What's the matter with you? You were up there, weren't you?" That was that. There were you and there was the windmill, and you had to fix it. The first time he called home, collect, his father told him not to telephone again until he could afford to. That is the character-building upbringing he had.

Both Jim and his father had what he described as a passion and temper that frightened him, so a great deal of energy was directed towards keeping the lid on it. I wonder sometimes what further might have evolved if this fear of passion could have been channelled constructively.

Jim's loyalty could always be counted on; his ethics, discipline and powers of concentration were all very finely honed. On my ranch he was a true blessing, and I feel enriched as a person for his crossing my path. When I asked him sometimes how he was, the answer would come as if from afar, "Still followin' that ol' cow". One sees in the genuine cowboy who still follows that ol' cow a great depth of observation and knowledge of land, cattle, wildlife and people.

But the same Jim who is so careful with cows and will lose himself with them, allowing each cow to have a separate identity within the herd, can never do anything but stand apart and watch the human condition. He had no time to experiment with girls when he was young, because he was too busy meeting the rigours of the elements on the Saskatchewan range. He regrets not having had that experience. He finds city slickers unacceptable, and the fact that they live in houses built close together (which they can't help) *unthinkable*. He is a great horseman, and his horses are interesting and intense.

One time during haying I asked him to cut a certain field, and could tell by his face that something was amiss in my asking. He would not say what, so I went to the field where he was working and sat in the long grass until he came by on the swather to cut the field, whereupon I asked what was troubling him. He entered upon a soliloquy about himself as a child sitting and listening to his father and the Indians. From them he had learned the importance of spring grazing; the young shoots grow between the old grass that gives extra milk to the cow so that she can feed her young, and that makes you money. This field I had asked him to cut was one he had designated to be left as old grass, so that the young shoots would come up amongst the old ones and be protected in the spring. When he told me this I asked him to stop cutting the field if he felt it was wrong to do so. He said, "No, I have to finish this round, or the field would look like a drunken Indian chasing a squaw." So I mounted the tractor to tidy up the field, and there was peace between us. Most people were jugheads to him, who thought only of winter feeding and summer pasture without considering the spring and fall.

Another time I asked him to burn dead wood that had gathered alongside the creek. He did not do it, and respecting his wisdom I said nothing. One day, long after, I was walking along the creek and saw him with a tractor and front-end loader pushing all the wood together. (This was in winter.) "My Indian blood tells me there's going to be a chinook [a warm Alberta wind that appears in winter and melts everything suddenly]. What does yours tell you?" he asked, and I said, "I wish I had more Indian blood". A bull camp was nearby, and Jim explained that had he burned the wood earlier the bulls, being cold, would have come down to the warmth of the ashes. Standing on warm ashes after hard snow, they would have become tender-footed, but with the chinook now imminent there was no longer danger in burning the wood, for there would not be that variation of temperature underfoot.

One morning he rang to say there were about eighty elk near my barn. The trouble is that elk trample the hay whilst feeding, and cows do not want to eat what they leave, because it smells of elk urine. Jim did not chase the elk out or frighten them in any way; he simply clapped his hands and told them, "Now get back to the woods where you belong" – and they did, for he has the gift of being able to control animals by his voice alone.

I learned from him how to find the right balance between tuning in and tuning out; cows like to calve where it is reasonably quiet, and they want to be alone, so the less human interference the better. "Watch them bunching up and then see a cow leave; if she don't mosey off slow, but is travelling fast, she's going to calve. You never find elk with other elk or buffaloes when they calve. It's only human beings who run to be together in hospitals to give birth." With cows, one should only intervene if the weather is very cold or if there is some other problem. Once interfered with, mothering up is never the same again.

Once during a warm, early February there was a sudden snowstorm. Jim told me that the stress of the weather changing would cause early calving, and he was right; that night we had seventeen births – on a normal night there are about four. In the morning he went out and located each of the seventeen newborn calves in the snow, then paired them up with their mothers (no mean feat). It was Jim who taught me that animals in pens are more restless if they are visited fitfully throughout the day than if someone comes in once a day and does all that has to be done. "Like you and me. If I know what time you're coming, I can settle in, but if I don't know what time to expect you, I can't settle to anything." And so, at times other than calving, Jim makes a tour of the cattle once a day.

He observed that animals amble and wander in curved walks from point of interest to point of interest; they walk and stop, walk and stop. If you want to catch a cow, you should also walk and stop, walk and stop, then you won't get it unsettled. He is also aware of the steady push of continual stress, on the cows as on himself.

Jim is as perceptive of people as of animals. A neighbour rang once to tell me that seven of my cows were in his field. I had often been pestered by these people, who resented my presence, calling to say that one cow had strayed to their field. Where Jim came from, people wouldn't bother each other but simply move the cows back, while this phone call meant that he had to take his dogs and ride for three hours.

Finally he arrived, only to find that the cows and their calves were not mine, they had a different brand. He rode the animals into the neighbour's corral, thinking to himself – as he told me later – "Let him explain to their owner how they got there". The neighbour came down to the corral and wanted to chat, but Jim would not: "I would have lost everything I had gained if I had stopped and had a friendly word with him. I just looked at him and said, 'Dave, I have to get much closer than a kitchen window to read a brand, I don't know about you.' Now," he said to me, "that man will act like a white man, and when he has one of our cows he will put it over the fence like any white man would do." I have never been bothered by these neighbours since.

Jim believes that a man who has a pen-and-paper job is a superior animal to one who labours all his life among earth and blood and dung, yet how much have I learned from him. He taught me about rotten snow and rotten ice. Northern children playing and leaping from floe to floe can read it. Sometimes you come upon a deceiving ice crust, and if you don't spot it, and make the mistake of stepping on it, you sink way down, deep below. The crust of ice that covers the crumbling snow and ice is to him like a bluffer in a man.

He taught me that when you felt hoarfrost underfoot, there would soon be pack ice. And so it was with cows and people. When he sensed something slippery in a person, or a troublemaker in a cow, he was much more wary than I was, and would quickly cull the cow or cut the person out of his life before trouble set in. One of his sayings is, "Behind every wild cow there is a wild man."

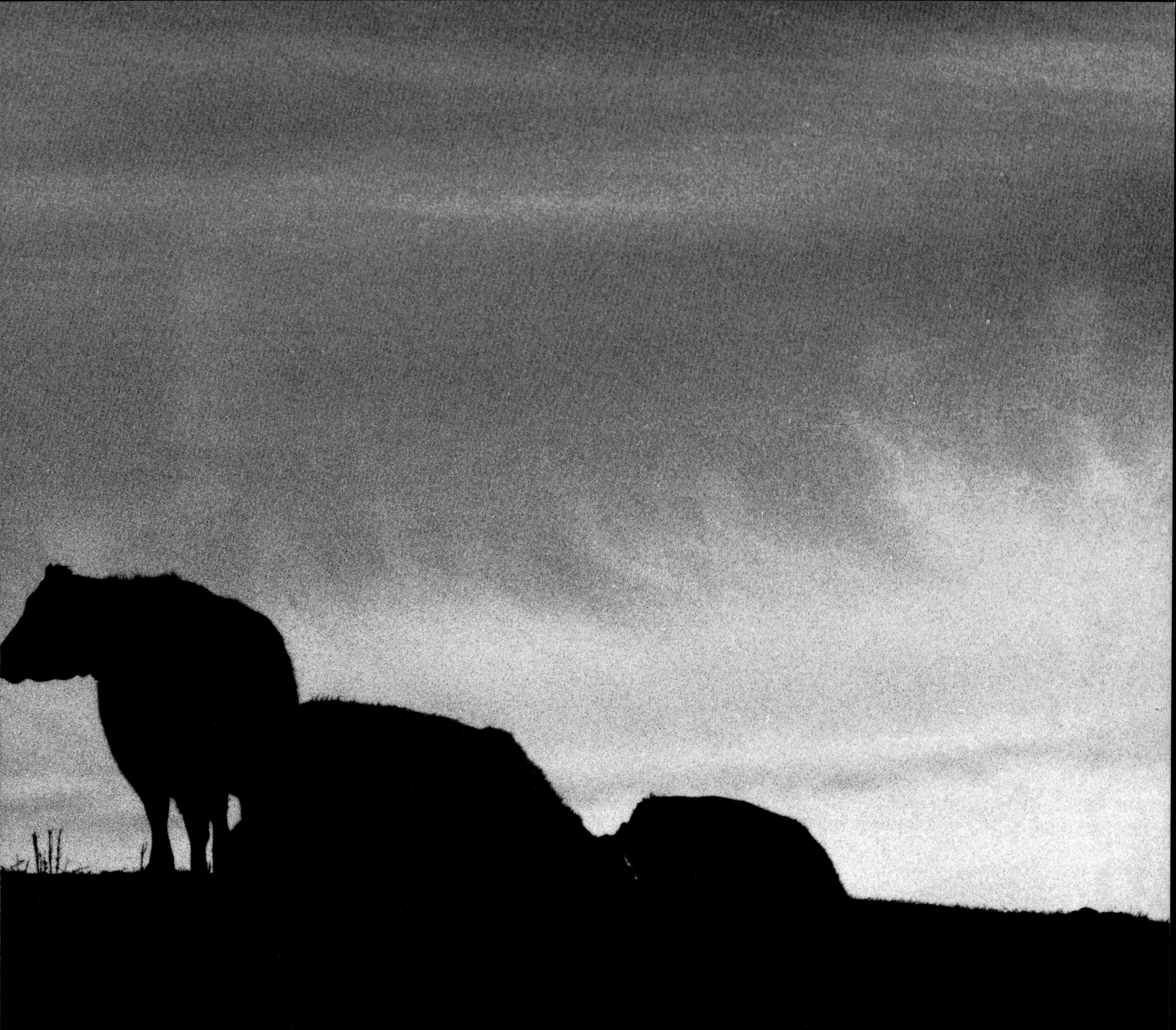

My corporate neighbour seemed to treat my land as an extension of their plant. Jim reversed their psychology, and ensured that when they came on to my land they were well aware whose land it was. Even the telephone company, when they came to look for wires, had to ask first. Jim looked at me with one of his lovely smiles and said, "I've run out of feudin' neighbours, I'll have to find another feudin' neighbour."

He felt deeply the intrusion of pipelines and well sites on our land. He once said, with great hurt, "Why don't they take the Alberta Heritage Fund (oil revenue, government fund) and buy Caterpillars and go up and down this country and ruin it all at once, instead of bit by bit?" He was a great support in helping me guide the oil companies into a greater understanding of our land.

CBC wanted a story about my dispute with Big Oil. I was shy of publicity, but Jim said he would go on TV. I watched as he went round on the tractor pondering what to say. The film crew arrived, all urban rush, and Jim came to me quietly and said, "It's not going to work." I knew what was bothering him; he called them slickers, urban people who did not fit into the rural sense of time and were in too much of a hurry to get to know a man. I faced this crew and told them, with all the fire I could muster, "It would take you years to plumb the depths of Jim Commodore, and if you cannot slow up, get down the road."

He was given double time on TV after that, not just locally but right across Canada, and one of the things he said was, "I have seen civilizations do without oil, but never yet seen them do without eating." He once came to an oil company meeting in town. As he walked through the door he saw at once that the best spot for him was between the head and the hatchet man, so he found himself sharing a sofa with the latter. Later he told me that when I spoke you couldn't see a thing on the corporate mask beside him, but he could feel the sofa where he sat jumping.

Jim was astute about government, environmentalists and all the officials who came to the land, to count coyote or for whatever other reason. "Their luggage lives in town. Their suitcases live in town. They cannot know how a coyote feels." He was very protective of me, saying, "You may not see the people you want to see as much as you want to see them, but you'll never see the people you don't want to see."

A typical ranch day he saw as one big mismanaged crisis after another. "The only thing that wanted to start on the place was my alarm clock."

But as Jung wrote, "Every good man has a shadow". Jim's was manifest in his ever-present prankstering, which to me usually bespeaks a deep sense of desperation. He devised prank situations to show up others, to bring out their "jugheadedness".

A mild test was his appearing before 8am one day all dressed up, with a smart cowboy handkerchief wrapped neatly around his neck, to find me drowsily still in a bathrobe, the ploy being that whatever he had on his mind would issue forth as crisply as his dressed-up self, to be answered by a still sleepy me. The best way of dealing with this, I decided, was to get up even earlier, a day or two later, and meet him in the corral, where he was still unshaven, with none of that town "get-up" on. Without a word said, we agreed we were quits.

Jim was the high point of the many cowboys who have worked for me. Most of them were good, but although everyone adds something, there were others who were not easy men, restless, dissatisfied, always pursuing a dream which would never become reality. In some patients mental psychosis takes the form of imagining they are Jesus Christ, but nowadays it can also manifest itself through the romantic idea of "becoming a cowboy", and in the psychiatric ward of a London hospital I have seen young schizophrenic men loping along with a cool cowboy walk. In our big cities, and even in Germany, Japan and England, groups meet together to wear their cowboy gear, share cowboy catalogues and eat cowboy food. There is even a black group in Brooklyn. Fortunately the Canadian landscape provides a big enough canvas to act out one's madness, so the occasional "con cowboy" who appeared on my ranch has done so harmlessly in the form of a tinhorn or two.

After some years Jim left me to work for the PFRA, as his father had before him. And now, he declares, he is getting old and complacent (for complacent read lazy, he says). "Things don't seem as serious now as they did a few years ago." There has been a further winnowing and of knowing what really matters in life. The man who once told me that the most beautiful sight to his eyes was a herd of 1,600 cows strung out over two miles now cares for 3,000 cows on 1,600 acres, "and all I have to do is keep an eye on health, grass and water". He couldn't live in a street for the world.

Still followin' that ol' cow.

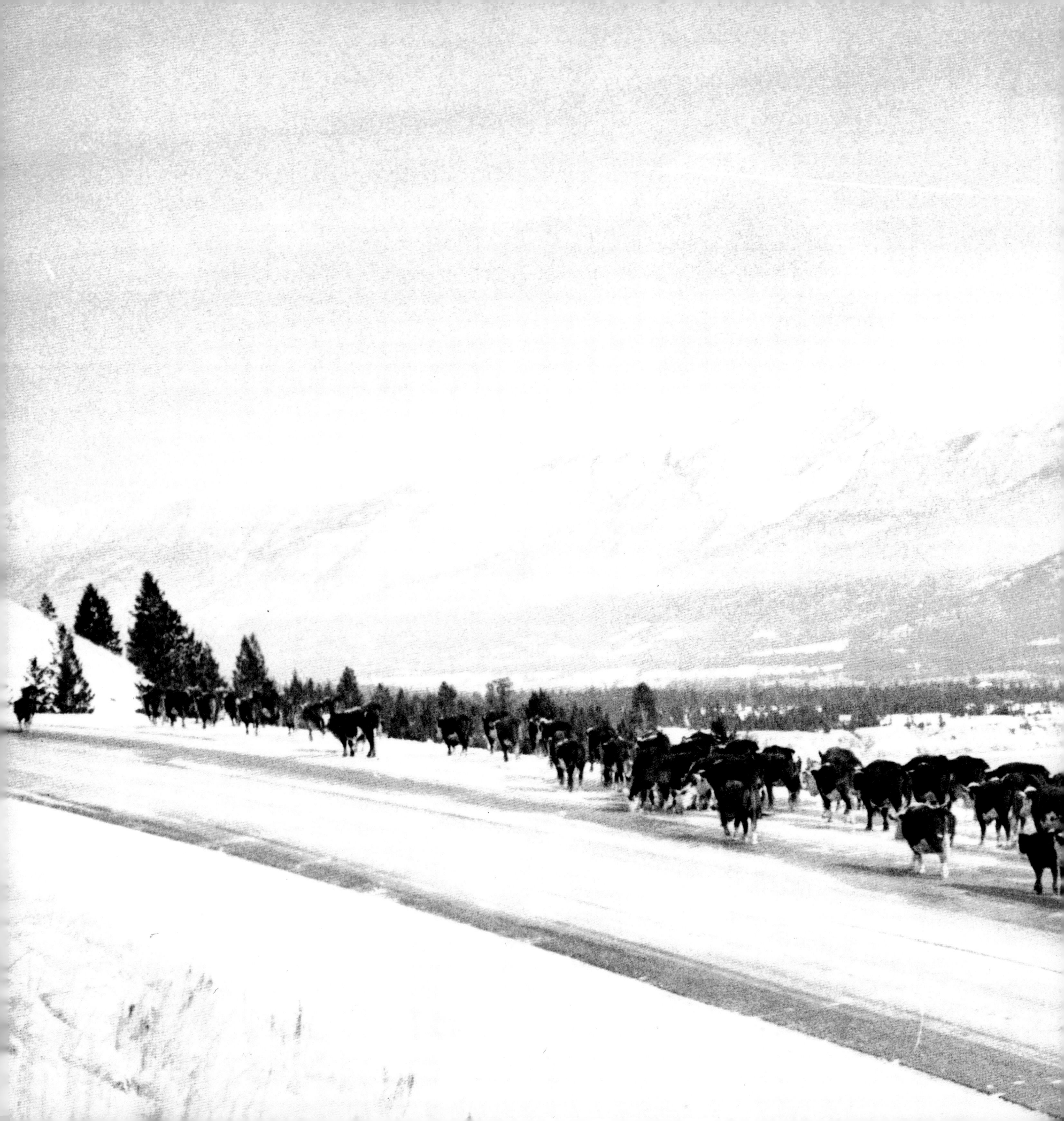

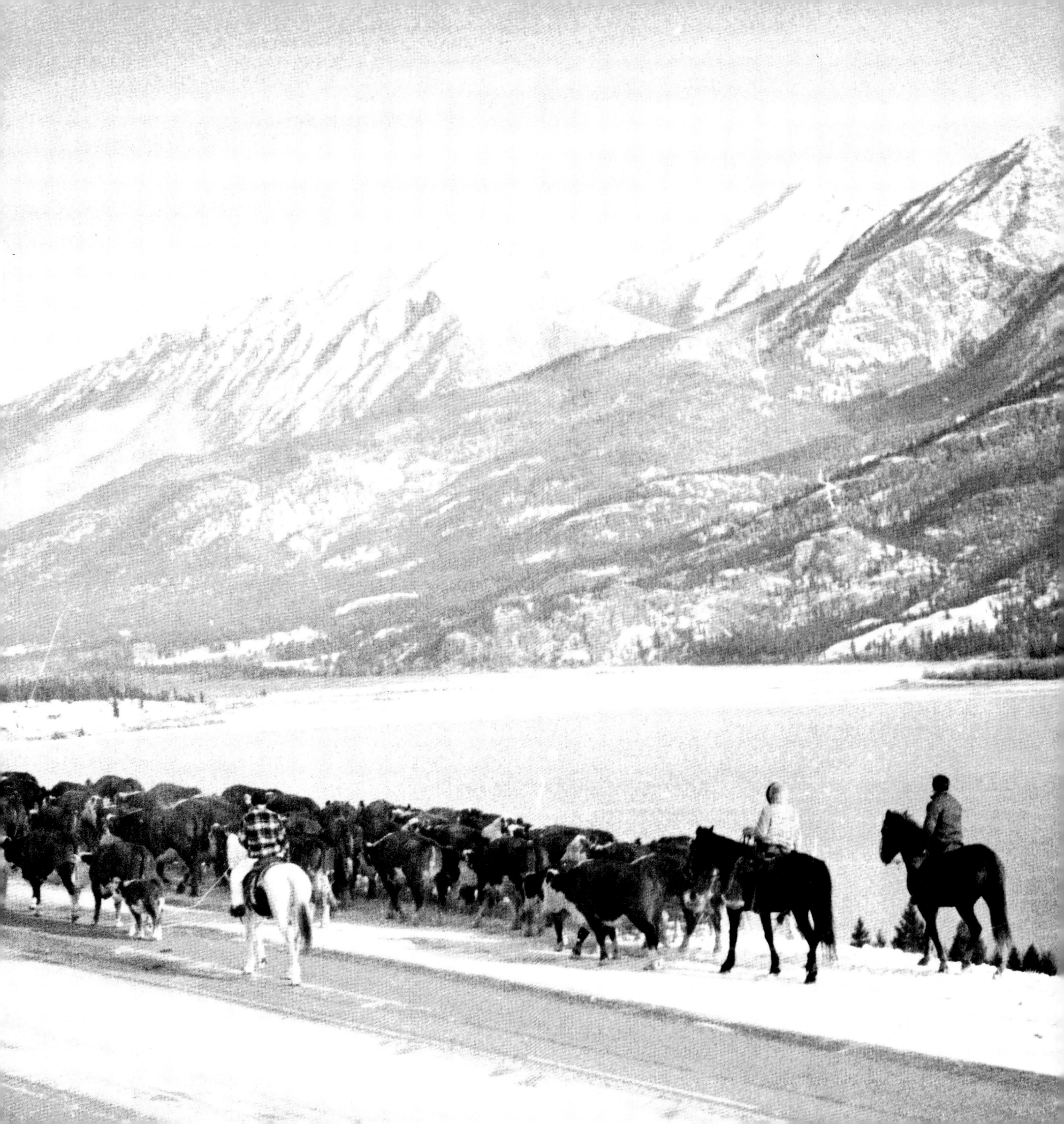

I come this morning and perch on the front step, a glass of tea in my hand. Facing me is a blue bird, sitting very still on a branch almost level with my sight line, and I stay with her stillness. Whilst I focus on her she focuses on me, but when I am distracted by another bird she flies away to a higher branch.

Today I am lucky enough to have as my companion Mabel Commodore, Jim's mother, who has come from Saskatchewan to visit her son. Now old, she was always caring and competent, and took over when her husband was flat on his back for a year and a half. On the twentieth anniversary of her husband's death she said to me, "Curly was tall and dark, and he treated me well." We have comfortable talk together as we enjoy the silvery light, the morning sun, the delicate early shadows.

This spring one, or sometimes two, bald eagles sit in a tree near the house. It is very unusual for them to come so near. Jim's mother has never seen a bald eagle before, and she follows them across the field as they fly high overhead, in her excitement almost becoming airborne herself.

The boughs are still bare and the trees leafless, but nest building is in the air. Each year one wonders how the birds manage to fly here from far-flung places like Brazil; some will stay and nest, but others will fly on to the Arctic. The same group of three Canada geese has arrived. They were here last year and the year before that. I believe one has lost its mate and that is why they are grouped thus. Canada geese mate for life, and it's sad when one of a pair is shot. Their loyalty to one another is like Mabel Commodore's to her husband.

We found a beautiful rock in the creek; it's almost square. Very rare. This is my morning for square stones – I have found a second one! I place my heavy finds on a grassy bank beside the creek, to admire them and retrieve one extra special stone on my way back. Teilhard de Chardin, a twentieth-century Catholic theologian, tells of the withinness of God in each stone, and how each has its own story.

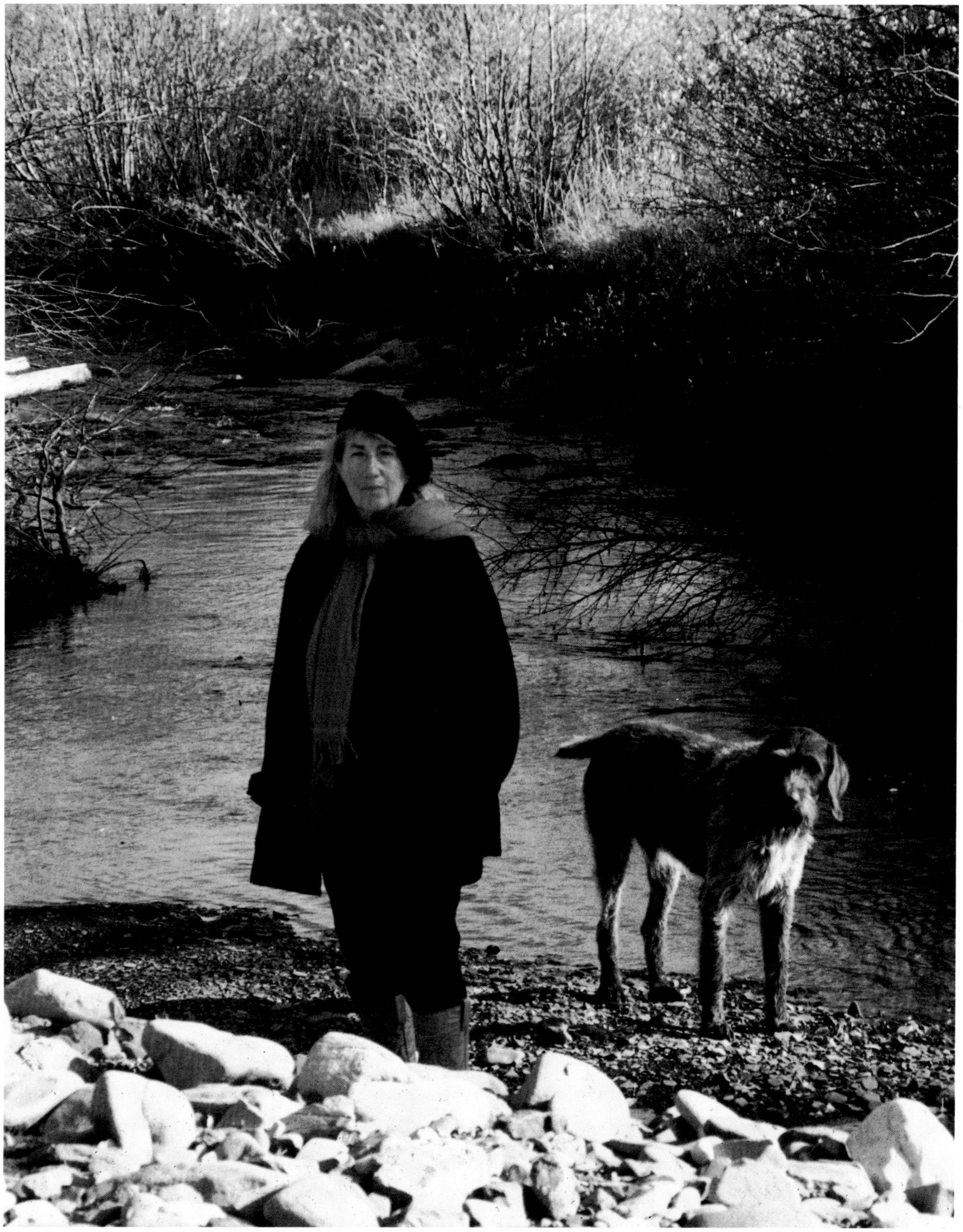

The Natives, too, live their lives knowing the withinness of stones. They take them for their ritual baths, pouring water over heated ones to create steam, but they use them only once in this way, and then return them to the creek with thanks to God. The Natives understand the livingness of the stones, and know that over-use will cause them to disintegrate.

The toes of the pussy willow branches are falling on to the creek water, snow-like, and the willows, as they lose their furry toes, are gaining fresh green shoots. The new grass is pushing through the earth, and for the first time this spring I can smell its emerald green. The grass is tender but also strong, for each blade has to make its way through the heavy clods of earth and must be resilient enough to survive if it is trampled on. Every blade of grass is a miracle.

I cross the creek on a log and fall in – my first creek baptism – and the cold is tolerable, getting a bit off the ice edge.

You do not know what chatter is until you have heard a squirrel trying to chase Bucky away with his chit-chat-squawk-squeal.

Bucky is very male in his protection of me – not just a friend, as a female dog would be, but a true protector. Wherever my energy goes he goes too, and if he senses that a creature is disturbing me, he is right at their heels; if he senses that I love a human or animal, he comes gently close to them and leans the side of his face against their leg. He gets really close, as close as they will allow, and sometimes he will stay like that when they move. As they move, he moves too, staying with that position, and it is quite funny to see his head and the other's leg moving in a new union.

There are two old manurings of coyote here, so they also like this opening in the grove. They probably lay right here on the spot where I am lying now. So we have the same taste in terrain – I feel quite good about that.

I mark as my territory, in spirit, the territory they have marked. Lying down and looking into the sun I see sunspots, orangey-red sunspots with a beautiful magenta in the middle. There is light and shadow on Bucky and me, and the reflection of a branch on my leg, so I feel very much part of nature and not a looker-on. I have light and shadow on me and within me. Jim Commodore would understand this, for he used to say that life wouldn't be worth living if he couldn't sit back each day and look at it.

I have been nipping off the tiny first shoots of dandelion leaves to eat because they have so much green in them. Along the bank where things seem to be more advanced I breakfasted on my first dandelion flower, and the edges of balsam poplar leaves; the pine syrup oozing out of the buds is the essence from which Friar's Balsam is made.

A carpet of wind-blown, long-ago pine cones and fresh, daring blades of grass, bits of baby clover, strawberry leaves, dandelion leaves, twigs of pine branches blown off by recent winds. A rough but gentle carpet underfoot for bare feet. By chance I found one tiny metal staple in the grass. How could it have got there? It could have upset some poor creature's inside.

Just one branch of willow. There is a yellow base of long main stem, and each small stem branching off turns into rust, and the tips of each shade into red.

Bulls

Jim and I agreed not to buy any bulls that were brought to the local bull sales, which usually take place in the spring, because these animals have always been overfed on grain; they look huge and impressive, but when they reach the ranch they suddenly lose all this weight which they have put on for auction and become unfit. A rich diet such as oats, barley, beet pulp and alfalfa cubes, which they are given specifically for the sale, is detrimental to their reproductive capacity: the libido, the quality of semen and the sperm reserves are all reduced. You get excess fat on the neck of the scrotum, and it impairs the thermoregulation of the testes. Commercial cattlemen sometimes go for looks and pay a higher premium on fat bulls, but the fact is they have a higher probability of being reproductively deficient. So we went out of our way to find working bulls that had not been given extra feed, and usually we bought them during the coldest weather, so we knew they were good ones and would be able to cope with the worst conditions.

I have often heard men get hung up by a gigantomania – huge bulls with long straight backs and not too thin in the pants (i.e., with fully muscled hips). It is impressive, I suppose, to see a big bull, but some of them have been so raised on the principle that bigger is better that to see them gives me a sense of discomfort. It is the character that draws me. One's character is one's fate; and just as with the rest of us, so with a bull. What is important is first and foremost a bullish character. Apart from this, one looks for a bull with good feet, for in order to be able to cover the range after the cow he needs good feet actually to mount that cow.

The University of Alberta suggested that we should not make our bull calves into steers, that is, castrate them. This requires an awareness of the problems of bull management, and of the fact that an effeminate bull, in cowboy parlance "a sweet-arsed bull", will be persecuted and ridden by the other, more masculine bulls, sometimes hounded literally to death.

Of course, one is seeking bullish character. The odd bull with his effeminacy, or the odd cow that is less than feminine, still keep their masculinity and femininity. The North Pole has not become the South Pole. The bull that is soft and the man who is sensitive are still being so in a male way, just as the cow that is bossy and the woman who is hard are still behaving in a female way. Cowboys always compare cows to ladies they know.

There is an inverse relationship between dominance and sexual behaviour: the bull that is big on fighting does not always get on with breeding. It is best to mix all the bulls in the herd a few weeks before breeding, so that the social dominance is established.

Since they have been shut away in a bull camp it is odd that, when let loose, instead of thirsting for the ladies they spend days working out seniority, the law of nature ensuring that the progeny are sired by the strongest male.

There is no magic – it is just common sense; Jim Commodore came to work for me precisely because I did not have exotic cattle, because my cattle were average-size animals, and I had no intentions of turning them into beefalo (the result of crossing a cow with a buffalo).

The bull's scrotum is important, for an animal having a normal scrotum with a distinct neck has the best development. Large scrotal circumference and good potential sperm production go together. The genetic traits of good testicular size have manifested themselves in female progeny, so that selecting the right bull will improve the reproductive potential of the cow. A well-chosen bull will help the cows to have a higher conception rate, earlier pubertal age and calving ease. A good bull is important too because we have such a short season for breeding.

One bull can serve eighteen to twenty-five cows by nature's methods, but up to ten thousand by artificial insemination. Bulls used for this purpose rarely live beyond eight years. At the artificial insemination centres they are kept in runs that might be suitable for dogs, and they stand on concrete, because concrete is easier to maintain. But concrete and feet do not mix well. This results in a softening of their feet, and leads to their premature death. The bull's penis is electrically stimulated so that its semen is gathered. Men complain that these bulls are mean bulls, but they do not stop to consider *why* the bulls are so bad-tempered. Would they not also be on edge in such a situation? Bulls' hooves are not provided with the luxury of "trainers".

Having obtained the semen for artificial insemination, it is necessary to know which cows are in heat, and therefore in breeding condition. The Gomer bull is used for this purpose. The Gomer bull has been vasectomized, or sexually disabled, and wears a bag of yellow paint around his neck. He mounts the cow in the normal way, and in mounting transfers a splash of the paint to the cow's rear end. He is not able to impregnate the cow, but the cow in heat will be readily identifiable by her yellow behind.

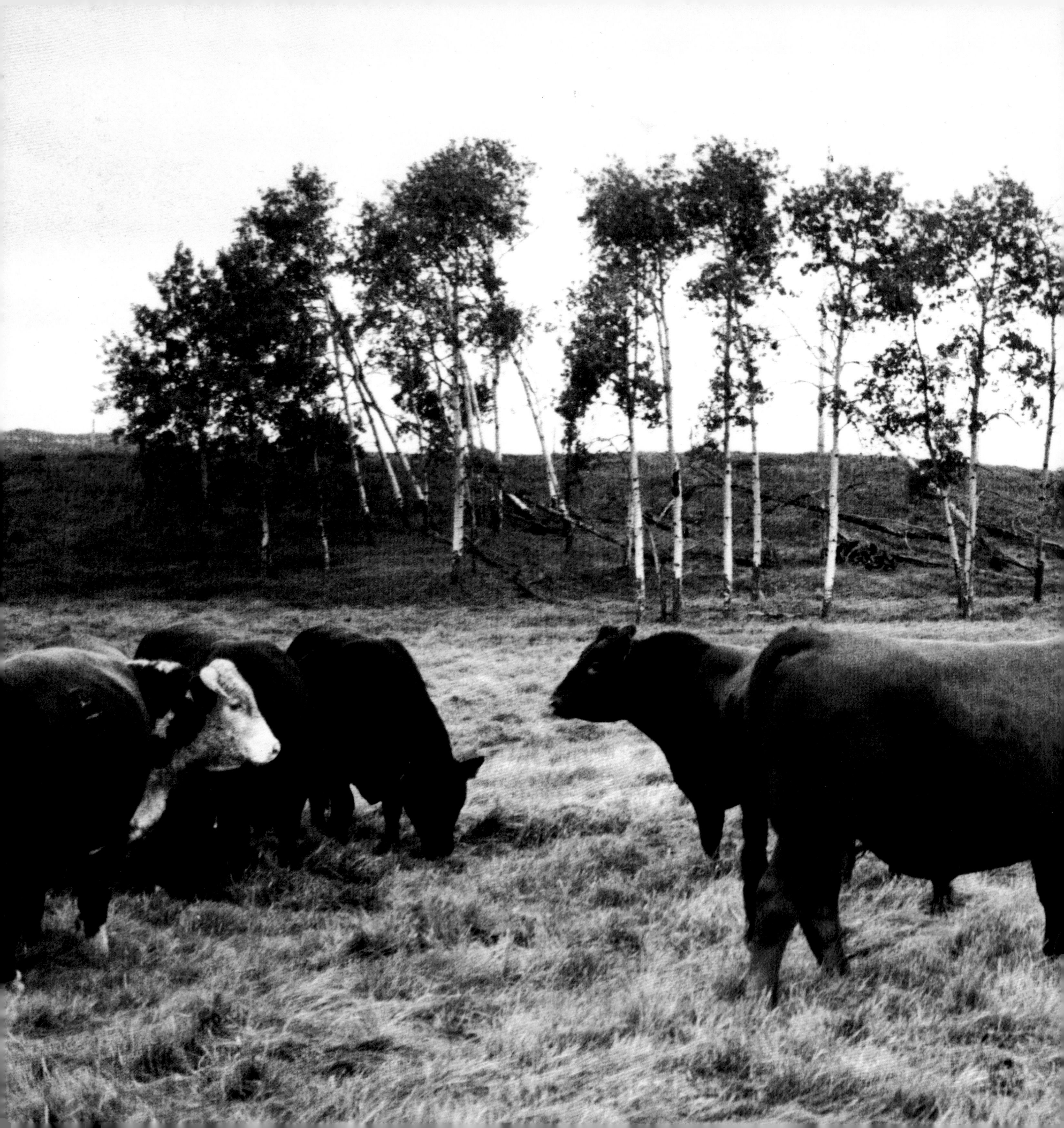

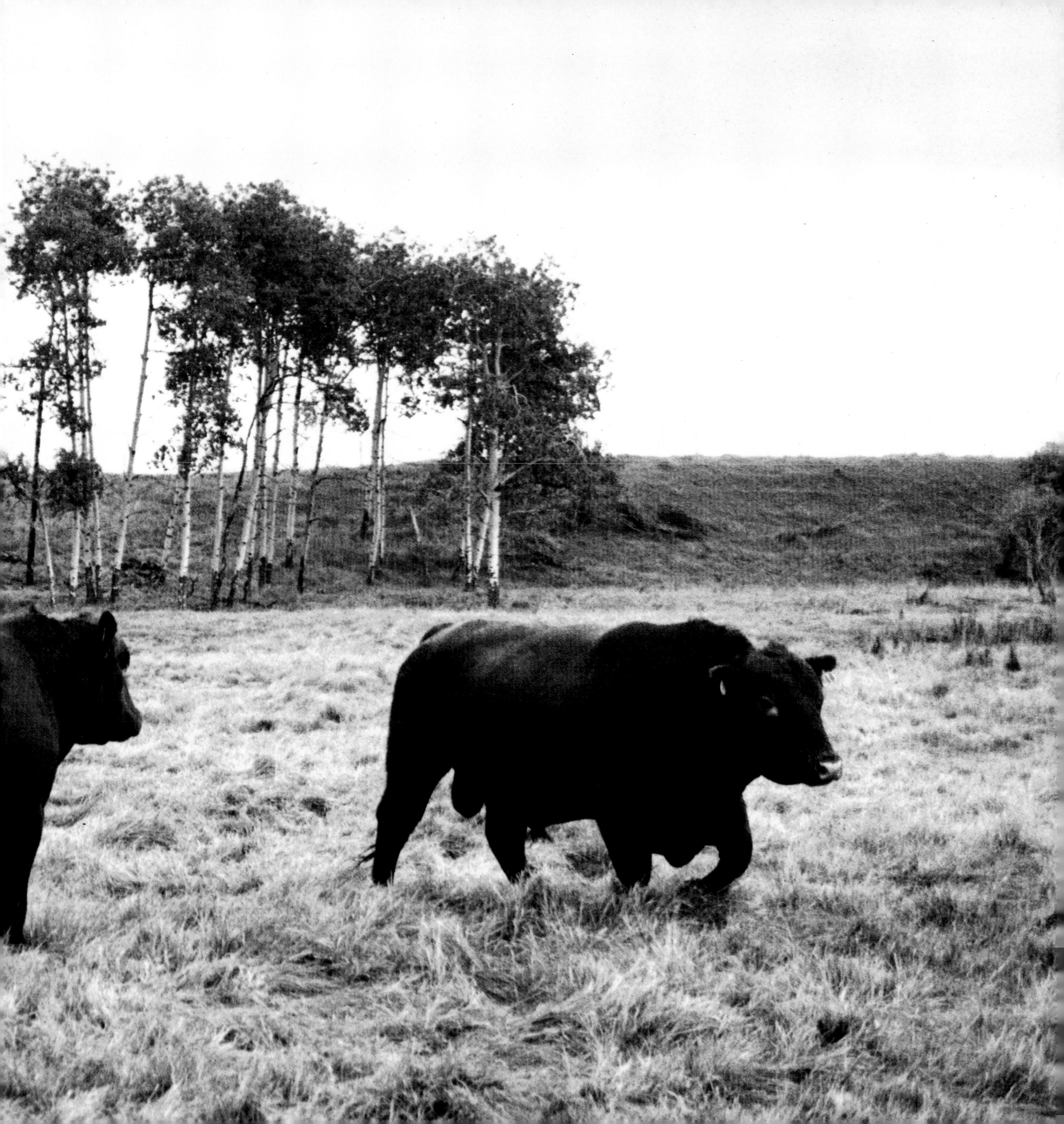

What concerns me is how much we interfere with nature. Some of the implements used to disable bulls from breeding are truly medieval – sometimes in the past, for instance, the bull's organ has been wrapped round with cement.

At times men use prods and whips far more than is necessary in moving cattle. Just as humans need to keep a social distance from each other, so with cattle. Cows have their flight field. If the animal is approached carefully and given its space, it will move along its own path, and can be eased to where one wants it to be. This takes longer than prodding and whipping, but I have always been amazed at man's ability to turn a blind eye to cruelty. It does not even make economic sense. How often does the free spirit created in the wilderness turn to wild wacko because of desperation and insanity? I have often asked myself that, when I see imbalanced inner stirrings being acted out on the land and its animals.

It has taken thousands of years to evolve cattle, and I feel we must examine our farming practices and consider whether we have the right to defy nature. For instance, it took thousands of years to get the right size of calf for the cow, so as to reach the udder – you cannot make big changes in one or two breedings. Can we not improve our farming methods so that we are able to succeed in the market place without all this? The more far-seeing ranchers are beginning to turn their thoughts to this matter.

I have never used artificial insemination. Grenadier, my first bull, came from Scotland, and I went there to choose him. A woman can read an animal as well as a man – it simply requires a tutored eye. In Alberta, buying a bull is generally thought to be cowboy country, but in Scotland there are women who are considered to be good herdsmen, and are thus accepted.

Ronan Nelson at Muchairn, Taynuilt, Oban, whose family owns the oldest Highland herd, had created from it a Luing herd. From his yearling crop he had chosen eight of his best bull offspring for me to look at. I chose the two I preferred, but as he had been there at birth I asked him to make the final choice. With animals, as with humans, the character is present from birth, and even though it may go under for a time, it will always reassert itself. So Grenadier was chosen, took an airplane trip, and came to live in Canada.

The hills of Alberta became his kingdom, and he taught me the true meaning of the word "pushover" as he cleared fences out of his way to make tracks on the earth as he knew he was meant to do, roaming free without boundaries. Sturdy corrals were mere stage sets and no impediment to his travels. He knew his dignified self was not to be boxed in any open-air ghetto.

I was told I was the only one to keep a bull as a pet, for Grenadier would mumble at my front door as he went roaming in the dusk. He was both aggressive and tender. He put a lot of competitive energy into being top bull on the ranch, but I would often find him in the dawn light lying restfully surrounded by a lot of baby calves.

I would visit him from time to time and just stay with him in the same field and be still. I was always mindful of the way animals spend hours patiently standing and eating rhythmically, and into this field of harmony would come a rush of human hurriers, on horseback or with a truck, because they wanted to move the herd elsewhere or market it.

Kim, my first dog, who sometimes came with me on my herd visits, was in a quandary in the early days, when the animals would approach closer to me and lick my feet – for she had been trained not to bestir the herd. How was she to protect me if she could not bark them away? I could feel confusion in her body, and then she would throw her whole self on my lap as I sat in the field. They, the cows, might lick my feet, but no further were they to go, for her body was a buffer between them and me.

When Grenadier found his way to a neighbour's land, it was with ease that I could tell him to make tracks back home – simply on foot with a stick in my hand which I rarely used. I would say, "Get on home, Grenadier, there are lots of ladies there", and he would move off waving his head back and forth and emitting much grumbling, but never losing his dignified self.

He insisted on being chief of the bull herd, and there he has remained all his life long. The early days were very busy; and now he is an old man, even though he can't make out with the ladies or be creative any longer, he still insists on trying to mount them and chase the other bulls away (how like a man!) – to the chagrin of my manager, who feels he is not contributing to the increase of my herd.

Yesterday I arrived at my secret spot to find the rising of land mists. It began like that, a walk through mizzle (a mixture of mist and drizzle), and then I could go no further because I was actually walking into water. The melting snow running down from the mountain peaks was so abounding that it filled the creek and even flooded my secret spot. Once in winter when it was 40° below I could not go there, and now again I could not reach it. Special places, precious people, are not always accessible or available.

As I back-tracked, this part of the Bible came to me:

For in the wilderness shall waters break out,
And streams in the desert.
And the parched ground shall become a pool,
And the thirsty land springs of water:
And a highway shall be there, and a way,
And it shall be called "the way of holiness".

I thought about this highway as the path through the secret spots in my book, this path which gives one a sense of direction. It leads to no goal, it doesn't show you where you are going, but it gives you a sense of knowing when you are on the right way.

Today I try again, a circumnavigatory route this time. I approach from a different direction by way of an old animal path, curved and winding, which leads to higher ground. Sometimes it takes me under bushes, a little too close to the earth for my height.

Arriving there, I seek a level where it's not flooded. A tree leans over, its upturned roots washed by the flood waters. It may withstand the water flow and recover, or it may float away and end its days.

I find a bit of dry land and make my way to my tree sit. There's actually a substantial waterfall coming right through a part of the earth's surface. Just standing under this tree trunk, I see three huge waterfalls. The quiet secret spot that was just a little rivulet of water, barely running, now has strong water in three different courses feeding into it. It's become a huge, wide, alive, coursing stream that has flowed down from the mountain tops.

To crawl into a badger hole, up to my knees, inadvertently; to have bitter herbs and sweet herbs; to know the water course – all in a short morning walk…And Bucky is alive with it – the intangible water force has manifested itself in his body and he's bouncing around with it. He's an energy factory, and I've leapt over a stream which would have been impassable before – all from the same creative force.

The Hebrews and Egyptians had a true sense of water; in it they saw the God of Life who springs from the inundation of the mountain snow and dies down with the heat of summer.

The waft of silver willow scent – I am exalted by waves of fragrance, waves of water, flights of birds, flurry, scurry, of gophers leaping. And Bucky and I are somewhere amidst all this movement. I feel elated by the idea that standing on the ground, listening to the rhythms of the earth and the celestial music around us, is a form of prayer. Isn't praying listening to God? The earth rises into land mist, the heavens rain, and it is in this misty area between heaven and earth that we are in the pure numinous present and see many layers of universe reconciled. Happiness is here…inherent in the moment.

As I walk on I see the forest behind my secret garden all awash. I have never seen such a shift, not since I've known it. Everything is washed out, ready for rebirth. I suppose that's what I am too – about to be reborn. I discover an inner sacred circle formed by the trees. In this circle in the midst of growing they have twined their roots, appearing as a couple, a triplet, a quintuplet tree family, like five seeds in an apple. A few days later the sound and thrust have gone. The flood water has subsided, leaving an ocean of mud. As the wind blew patterns in the winter snow, so now it has blown similar traces in the mud.

God has totally washed the past and purified it. There will be a lot more regeneration of trees, because the seed harvest of pine cones that the squirrels gathered for winter has been washed into the holes in the earth which they created for their hibernation.

Great hopes for my secret spot after this heavy rain. Later on it will be fascinating to watch nature's effects. Shall I compare myself to this wood? It will be interesting to follow our mutual growth.

Andy Russell

Andy came into my life to help me put matters right with regard to Big Oil, shewing great loyalty when I was on my own. In the past he had been the only person to fight the oil companies, having led fifteen ranchers in the south in their crusade against a major oil company. Unlike the oilmen, Andy didn't scoff – he thought I was quite a girl! So began our friendship. He saw my capacity for careful strategy, and stood alongside when others faded fearfully away. He hung and rattled with me throughout my great battle – I was the general, he said, and he was the field marshal – and for this I owe him an enormous debt of gratitude. I was drawn to him too because of his identification with Beginnings.

Andy's face is very much like the face of a Native Indian: it gives the same impression of having been chiselled out of rock, a mountain-man look. When you meet him you are aware of something very other than urban. He manifests a great presence, which is felt in the first moment of seeing him. He walks with a purposeful spirit, and when his legs move they show much time spent snow shoe-ing; there is a rhythm to it. Natives often say to him, "I don't know whether you're Indian or white man".

His motto for life was given him by his father, who broke wild horses. The horse would be bucking with frenzy at the new experience of a rider on its back, and Andy's dad would tell him, "Hang and rattle, son. Hang and rattle." So he has the real "stick-to-it-iveness" of learning to go with a bumpy ride in life. He also has the timing, knowing when to jerk the rope of life, as when reining in a horse. Dealing with oilmen, he declared, was like breaking in a horse with a halter; the horse strains at the halter and tightens the rope on itself. You loosen it, and the horse talks to you. Oilmen, he said, were the same. From his mother he learned another skill. All cowboys can sew, because they can turn their hand to anything, but Andy's mother also taught him, as a small boy, to do embroidery.

Andy became a trapper whilst still in his teens, and long years in the mountains of Alberta developed in him strong powers of observation and an empathy with wild creatures and their habitat. The difference between a trapper and a cowboy is that the trapper has an understanding of the need for watching and waiting. "What's the tearing hurry?" he will ask someone in a rush. "You get nowhere in a tearing hurry." Like an animal hunting its prey, Andy has the ability to wait with total concentration and patience while waiting is necessary, and the instinct to know when the moment for pouncing has come. He is also a great tracker. One of his more disparaging comments about somebody was, "He couldn't track an elephant in a pile of shavings." He sees not only tracks on the ground, but animals around him that are invisible to other eyes.

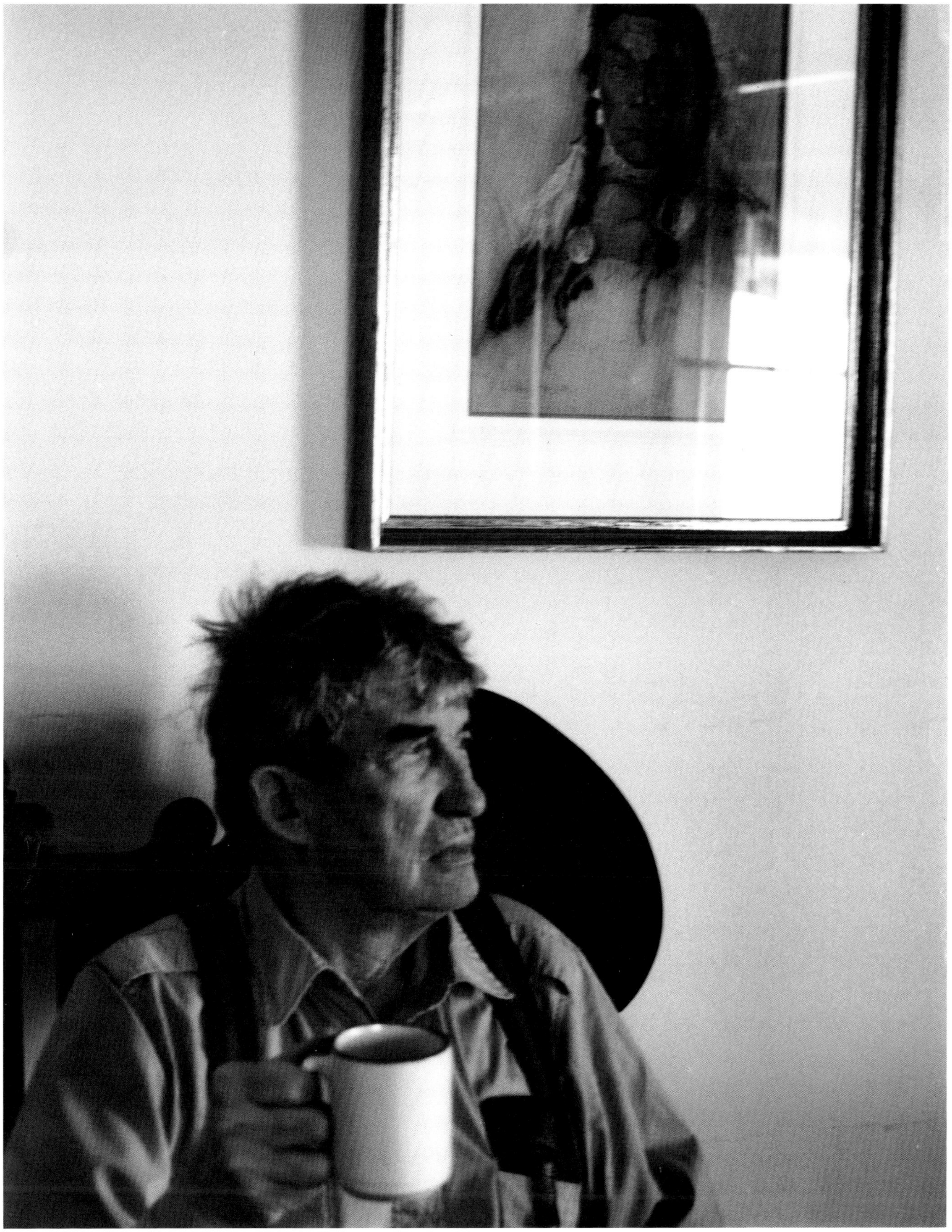

Fame originally came to him through his understanding of the coyote, though he is now best known for his work on grizzly bears. Having observed that everything runs from a grizzly bear, and the bear is always faster, he proved that you have a better chance of survival if you stand still and allow the grizzly to walk down another path. It requires great courage and self-confidence. This standing still in the face of adversity is something he does well.

His sense of oneness between himself and all other creatures is most poignantly illustrated when one observes him in a big city. When I saw him during a trip to London, he was largely silent. I enquired if that was because he was watching (he does a lot of watching in Canada) and he replied, "I'll never give up watching. I've never been in cities before, and I have to figure them out." Was he lonesome for lack of animals? On the contrary – I was amazed to learn how quickly he had placed himself in relation to the few around; from the sixth floor building he had noticed the squirrel houses in the trees below, and he remarked that this was the first time he had lived *above* the birds rather than below them. He wondered, too, about the mountain that had been sliced down to provide paving stones for London's streets. He looked at this unfamiliar urban landscape as if he were on the moon, with the same curiosity and freshness of vision. But if he is alone in a city, or on unfamiliar territory, he is lost. Even Calgary is "too much city", and not till he is back on the road to home does he feel able to breathe freely. On a train journey to Scotland, where he was being met at the other end, he was totally disorientated, and disappeared for two days.

A cameo of history came with the interplay between Andy and Joe and Josephine, the Crowshoes from the Peigan Reserve, who are the medicine couple of the tribe, and their friends of the same vintage (70 to 80 years old). All of us sitting together at the midway of Stampede Corral eating corn on the cob and potato chips, when one of the men said to Andy, "Our elders told us you wrote it the way it WAS", and Andy answered, "Yes, because I was in the mountains and you were on the reservation. Roaming free, I could see the way it was."

History flashed before my eyes at that moment. Andy's father was the first white boy born in Lethbridge, Alberta, and I realised that the Natives had been put on the reservations and had their boundaries limited at the same time as Andy and his father were free to ride the mountains as the Indians had once done. The ghetto-ness of the Indian reservation and their buffalo-less diet really hit me.

So we have the Native and the early white man meeting the land and its creatures freely and in a similar way – until the white man erected fences, and then the white man saw things the Indian on the reservation could no longer experience. Because the son became a writer and wrote of his meeting with the land, he and the Indians share a similar link. This was how he was able to portray in his books an image of a life others wish they had lived.

Andy cares desperately about flowing water. It is one thing for him to see land fenced, but to see water fenced makes him deeply sad, as if when a river is dammed he too is personally dammed.

All his life he has felt the need to prove himself. This has made him very competitive: he had to cast the best fly, tie the best hitches on a pack, shoot better than anyone else. The steps along the way have made the world a proving ground, not only in fishing and shooting, but also in boxing and guiding, and of later years in entertaining, story-telling, TV talks, public relations, making movies and writing. All these worlds he needed to conquer, to prove himself the best at all of them. And this he has done.

In the ten years of our friendship, I have got to know something of the man beneath this outstanding exterior – a shy, sometimes sensitive, sometimes exceedingly tough person who watched how the animal world works, and was able to make his way from trapper to guide to writer to environmentalist. Life is a series of waves and wavelets, a surge of energy to the crest of a wave, a talk delivered with great professionalism, and then a descent into the trough until the next speech. I have found, especially further north, that the hardier the life, the finer the type of person. It's a gift to be near Andy and people of his ilk, for there is a whole computer generation today cut off from experience of this kind.

Andy learned his behaviour patterns and relationships from animals. One of the things with which he is unfamiliar – for animals don't cry – is what he describes as "a woman clouding up and raining all over me". On such occasions he always waits for the cloud to lift off, but never feels any reason to meet the cause of the cloud. It is quite extraordinary that he does not converse much. His time in the woods was first spent watching people for the hunt, and then entertaining dudes as a guide; neither allowed for dialogue. You cannot get near an animal if you approach it directly; you must walk alongside and often walk away. So, too, does Andy never look at one directly, finding it painful to do so. He likes to watch unobserved.

I love going with a tracker who can read every sign on the earth's crust, and Andy is a pro. There is always a lot of tracking to be done on a ranch. One day I remember particularly, when we went out in search of a bear; Andy, Bucky and I. There was an autumn shortage of berries on the mountains, and bears had descended into the valleys looking for food. A cow had been shot and left by a "recreational" killer, and a bear had been eating it for a couple of days.

There were deer all over the place, but no sign of a fresh buck track. Sometimes, when a piece of wood bleaches, you can't tell whether it's bark, a stone, or a bone, but after a while Andy called out, "See here. Fresh buck track here!"

There was a squirrel trail on the log right in front of me. "See the tracks!" he said.

Evidence of a white-tailed deer – he jumped a fence, caught his tummy, left traces of hair. A hole in the base of a tree where a badger has been.

Andy said, "A mighty cold trail. We've caught a mighty cold trail. When you're looking after a wounded bear you have to take advantage of every little detail, or you get yourself killed."

We come across a track, and he surmised, "Big track. Cattle track? A dead cow, and the bear was full of it. He feasted on it for a couple of days and then headed straight for the mountains. Once he had his feast he wouldn't break stride until he got clear into the forestry reserve."

Then, pointing, he said, "Moose track – it doesn't show plain because it was made when the ground was frozen. Elk and deer and cow and everything mixed up here on the mud beside the creek – frozen mud."

Fresh deer track. Anybody can track in snow, but it was more difficult with snow cover off. So we never caught up with the bear.

At the time he was growing up there were no public libraries. A remittance man nearby had a library and a pad and pencil on string nailed to the wall. Andy could ride over and borrow a book, note it on the pad, and cross his name out when he returned the book. The drugstore in a nearby town had surplus magazines which were eventually sold off cheap. Andy could ride there and buy or be given these magazines. His uncle helped by sending a year's supply of the old *Saturday Evening Post*. In this Andy found the serialised saga of Andy Burnett, set in the 1800's and written by Stewart Edward White, the stirring and romantic life-story of a hero portrayed as one of the early pioneers opening up the American West.

When he was older Andy traced the trails of Andy Burnett in Montana and California and found the exact spots where he was said to have been. Telling me of this, he declared, "I have to say that when you read it you will learn something about life on the wild side where you depend on your two hands and your head – and your brains. It's never been the same since, and never will be again. I just know that. California's a pig-sty now compared to what it was then – beautiful country. I was out there – I travelled through those hills – west of Santa Barbara – over the mountains to the east. I've been to both, and both were described in Stewart White's books. The change in the prospects of the Californian civilisation was described in enormous detail by people who were there and I've given it to you, so that if you read it you will know what went on at that time.

"When I read about Andy Burnett," he went on, "I didn't talk about it, I wasn't aware of living it, I just *did* live it, I really did. There were mountains and rivers and horses, and it became my life."

It is easy to see why the legend of Andy Burnett caught his imagination. For a bold, high-spirited boy, brought up as he had been, his namesake represented everything he valued: extreme courage and fortitude in the face of danger; the ability to bear cold, hunger and deprivation of material comfort; far-sightedness and quick-wittedness (the certainty, for instance, of being able to draw a gun and aim faultlessly before your enemy even realised you were there).

Here was the life of adventure that he craved, with always the next mountain range to be conquered, and everywhere around scenes of wild beauty. Such a boy, and such a man as Andy Burnett became, must be a master of many skills, including hard-won knowledge of guns, horses, trapping, the ways of wild animals, and particularly of the elk and buffaloes on which his living and his life depended. He needed, too, to understand the ways of the Indians, an aspect of Burnett's tale which is particularly fascinating, since he was accorded the rare privilege of being initiated into the Blackfoot tribe. So later in life Andy Russell acquired all the skills necessary for this way of life: consummate shot, ballistics expert, showman flycaster, and with a fine sense of anatomy that enabled him to carve any beast well and to set broken bones expertly, human as well as animal.

When Andy takes parties into the mountains, he holds them spellbound with his tales of adventure, of what life was like in a world unfenced and unspoilt. And in the morning, over a blazing fire, he will make and toss a succession of perfect pancakes, starting the day once again as the brilliant entertainer, playing a role at which he is a master, and which enables him to share with others the essence of his own life.

Being the sensitive person he is, he was able to put into writing the world of Andy Burnett in the nineteenth century and of his own life in the twentieth. He projected it with his imagery for those later in our century who would never see unfenced land with wild life near at hand, kindling their imagination so that they would want to live as he had done. He internalised it, lived it, and through his creativity enabled others to experience the immediacy of the feelings he himself had. This is why barn horses, which have no experience of the wild, interest him little.

But the skills of trapping and hunting do not stop when one walks from the wild into one's abode. Those skills of watching and observing to de-stabilise an animal, so that it will go into the trap set for it, are sometimes useful in human social systems, and when in the midst of it one does not see it.

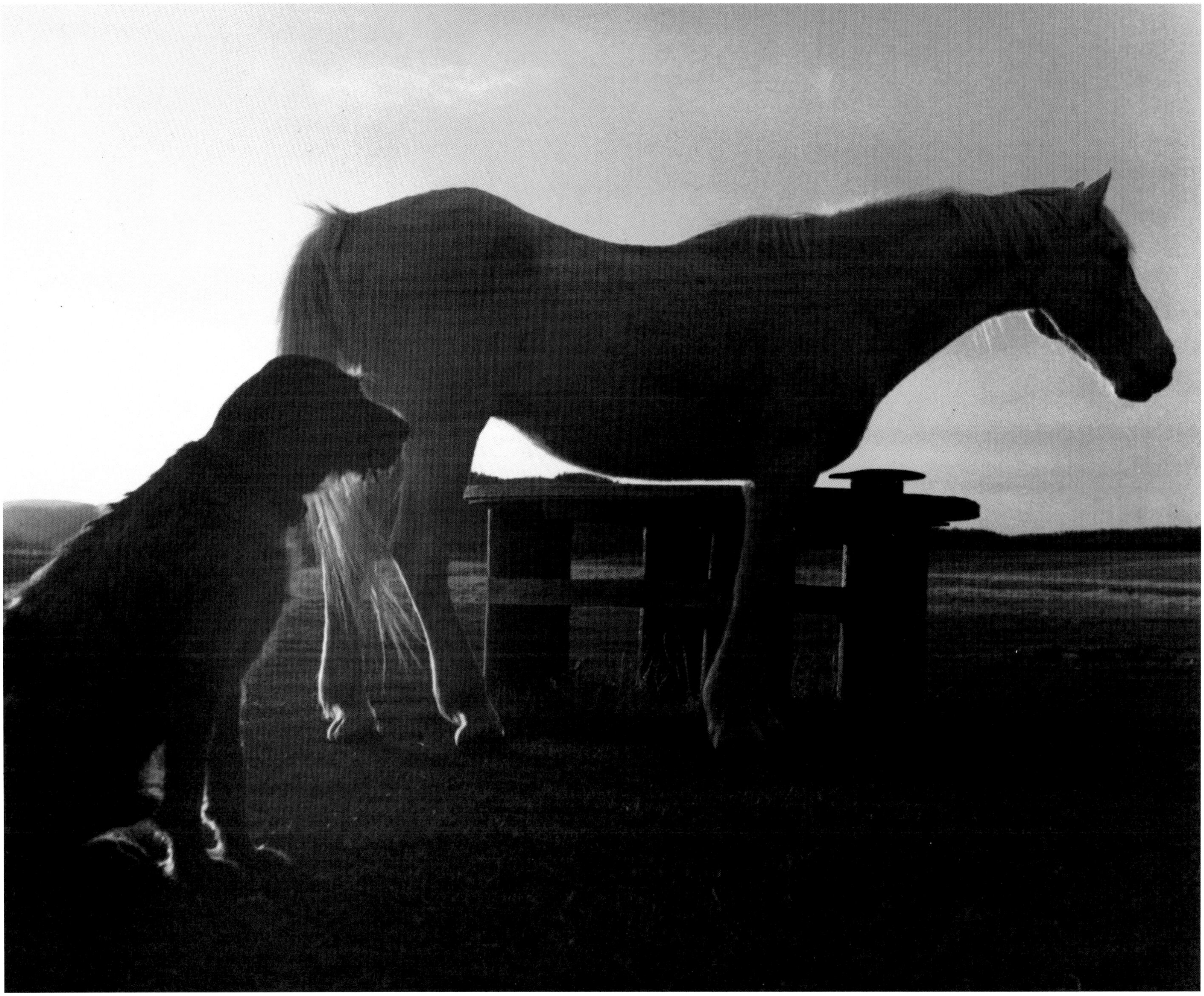

Bucky came to the ranch as Andy's dog, and because he had it made there he decided to stay. Here he lives in dog heaven. In dog heaven everybody is his friend, and he has the right and the freedom to go everywhere and never be denied the fun of running, smelling and sensing the universe.

He has no sense of scale; he tries to make love to a small cat, and is annoyed that when they play hide and seek the cat can hide in much smaller places than he can.

However, there is one foe right now in dog heaven – the manager's cow dog, Ben. Ben says "No!" to Bucky. Bucky cannot come into his (Ben's) yard or on to his (Ben's) truck. This denial threw Bucky into an uncontrollable rage, and they fought. The result was that Bucky hurt his paw and walked with a limp for a few weeks, while Ben hurt his mouth and couldn't eat for a while. There is still a good deal of mutual growling, and Bucky spends hours on one side of the fence glaring at Ben on the other, but this is a very small part of a beautiful life.

As he grew up, not only did he have all sorts of new animals to meet (cows, coyote, deer), but he would also chase butterflies. Now he's five years old, he has delusions of grandeur and chases birds flying through the air. Today a little coyote pup crossed my path and ran into the woods after Bucky's appearance and the accompanying yelps, but not with any great fear, more in fun as part of a game.

Whilst growing up Bucky was unsure of his dogdom; he would try to eat the horses' food, lie down when they lay down, and roll on one side when they rolled on one side. Ecstasy with Bucky is displayed in circular form as he runs alongside when I am on a horse. He goes around in circles when he's had some fun, such as spooking a coyote den, never in a straight line. I think ecstasy is in a circle.

Now Bucky has developed a technique for befriending the universe which works well and could be a model for us all. He stands still before any animal and allows it to sniff him all over, saying, "Here I am, take me as I am," until the animal knows him totally by his smell, and knows that he has nothing to hide.

He has a great ability to feel rage, mostly when he has been left out of something, and to remember and retain his rage. He will not respond to discipline if it humiliates him. He will not be treated like a dog, but responds to those who respect him and earn his respect.

Watching over me, Bucky is like a security officer, only much more fun. He stands or sits back in the woods behind a few trees, keeping me within sight. Sometimes he follows his nose, but even then I think he has a protective ear cocked my way. I can hardly see him, but he would be there if anyone bothered me. He would show that his jaw, which can hold a bird so tenderly, is also made for warfare. For the moment he oversees me from a distance, his head all hidden, resting on his outstretched paws.

Another aspect of Bucky is the great ham actor. He entertains me on my walks by circling round and round, holding wide branches in his mouth rather than the sticks and twigs favoured by other dogs. This year he does seem a little older, allowing things to be, not turning everything into doing.

A little white flower – I think it's called bear grass – and harebell I see on leaving my secret spot. And lots of equisetum (it means horsetail), which is a plant as old as the dinosaur and the birds. Morning light makes the tree trunks look so alive, even a felled tree. From a distance, I thought it might have been a big brown mammal.

I suppose the mushrooms are the miracle of this time in the woods – their silence, and the symbiosis that exists with the trees. The trees need them at their roots to help their breathing. The mushrooms push through silently, jewel-like in their colours and their deep, quiet beauty. Could we not, in the twenty-first century, in our inner cities where most people live, create a mushroom park, so that children who have been brought up on harsh twentieth-century noises of bleepers and blippers may stand away for a moment and learn again the secret of silence and stillness?

We stand on the earth, and in listening we pray with our feet. We listen to the music of the earth and the celestial music in the air around us. The earth rises into land mist and the heavens rain, and it is in this misty area, between heaven and earth, that we are in the pure present and see the many layers of the universe reconciled. There are trails on the earth, and star trails streaking the sky on a clear night. Happiness is here, inherent in the moment.

And God said, "Let there a firmament in the midst of the waters, and let it divide the waters from the waters. And God made the firmament, and divided the waters which were under the firmament from the waters which were above the firmament, and so it was. And God called the firmament, Heaven."

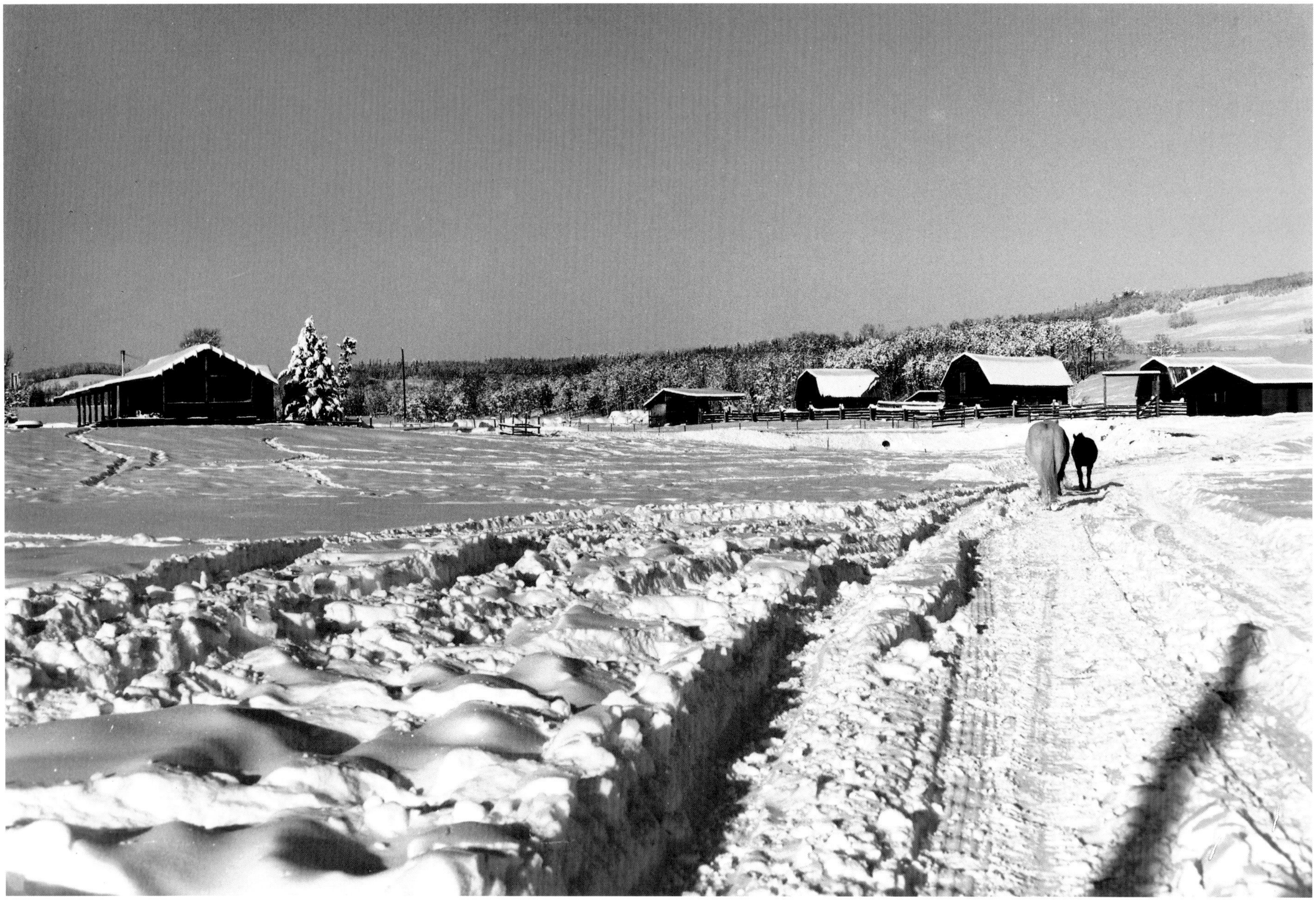

Breakfast at Rumsey Ranch – Swapping Stories

Andy and Jim Commodore have much in common. They would often swap stories at breakfast (there is no skulking behind newspapers at Rumsey), and I remember one such conversation in the winter of 1988, which for me was the most elemental in many a year. Jack Frost's ice painting gave the windows an extra glazing, and the doors of my cabin were framed with frost on the inside so that it needed a hefty tug to open them.

The bulls had got out, and calving was even earlier than we had planned. Imagine being outside with the temperature ranging from 35° to 47° below zero. Calves are born wet, and in these conditions must be dried off within two minutes, or they will be frozen and die, quite literally frozen to death. Jim brought in one such seemingly stiff carcase with unseeing eyes, and I took it into my sauna. Soon it was transformed into a beautiful calf with soft eyes, lying quietly in a bed of straw. He asked what would my society friends think of calves in my sauna – my answer was that I have no society friends!

Jim had returned to Rumsey Farm after an absence of ten years, which gave me as much pleasure as, I imagine, the return of the prodigal son gave his father. It was good for me, for Rumsey, and for Andy, too, who was writer in residence. Jim was sensitive to Andy. This was shrewdly assessed: "What Andy is looking for," Jim told me, "is involvement without responsibility." (Almost at the same time, not knowing of this remark, Andy had said to me: "What Jim wants is responsibility, but not too much.")

The following random snatches of talk, overheard from the next room one bitterly cold morning of this bitter winter, are fairly typical:

Andy: We undertook to take 250 head across in the storm. Oh, my God! I would never forget. The river had been high, like you say, and it froze. You could see rocks through the ice. It was slippery. Oh, man, we scattered hay and manure. We tried everything. Jack got the old milk cow and roped her calf and dragged it across. When it bawled, all the steers followed. *(Weather forecast on radio)* We'll live with it, though it didn't sound like the one I was trying to hear.
Jim: ...looking for dry cows. I keep thinking of Walt Larsen, "That cow has already proved she'd let me down." Walt never fed a cow. That country [Montana] has good winter grazing. In a snowstorm Walt, going through these cows, picked up a couple of dry ones. One cow, an awful nice cow, Walt says, "You see that cow up there? She calved in a snowstorm, she saved her calf. That's a good cow." He sure didn't have much trouble. He was merciless. Don't have both oars in the water, but they got her figured out...cows are better without us.

Andy: …crossed a river on horseback unwrapping a chocolate bar. This horse was real serious about it, if anything rattled it set him off real good. He would have liked to drown both of us. One old buzzard, the roughest, most miserable, hard-gaited son-of-a-gun, told Bert I didn't think it would make a lead horse. You know what he did? Tied it to a tree. Frank rode him. When he got back to the corral he wouldn't talk to me. It was fightin' and kickin' and snortin' with all the other horses. I got on the dirty devil, and he bucked over the bank and into the creek with his head out of sight; picks his head up, shakes his ears off, all of a sudden he decided it was easier to get along than buck with me again. With the lead horse you don't want a horse that hesitates, want him to stand his ground, otherwise every horse in the outfit knows, right now.

Jim: …had a horse that all of a sudden would squeal and come at me. I'd coil up a lariat and he would start. Finally it dawned on me what it was. I feed the tail of his rope down, I slowly let the tail of the rope down to his knees and then watch, and he'd buck. Took half the summer to figure that one out.

Andy: …had a wife. She quit him. Worked her to death. Ran into another woman, three in a row. One pulled out, two of them dead. Poor old guy. Drove you crazy, though.

Jim: I only met him a couple of times, didn't know him socially.

Andy: Good-hearted. Do things for people for no reason. Warm like an oven, smarter than hell, made a circle, light flashing. Two occasions got him out of a real jam. Couldn't say anything good about Vermont, so I gave him what for about that. "You're the damnedest liar I ever met." Just straight plain jealousy.

Jim: He's a good stockman.

Andy: He did pretty good with a herd of kids. A slug of them…the old fellow deserved more credit; he could be the 'orniest son of a gun.

Jim: Seems to me, maybe I'm wrong, always struck me as – I don't know why it is that the human species is the only one that congregates when giving birth.

Andy: The caribou and the dall sheep calve in a group.

Jim: But that's rather a community protection association – many pairs of eyes are better than one pair of eyes.

Andy: …(referring to Jim's hearing aid)…just like a TV set; you don't have to cross the room to switch things off…

Now Andy does a lot of porch-sits. "Time gets by a guy," he says. He watches animals as he has always done, his gun close by to pick off intruding coyotes, for his aim and his eye are still faultless. On a clear day, glimpsing the tips of the Rockies, he likes to scan the horizon, seeing elk, counting them, then verifying the numbers by gazing through his binoculars. Perhaps his moment of truth came once when he looked at Grenadier, old like himself, who has also done a lot of good for the world. There was, he felt, a kinship between them. When he dies he wants to be cremated and his ashes scattered on Beehive Mountain, because he has climbed it eighteen times.

Winter is swapping-story time, and "Breakfast at Rumsey" happened in deep cold. Now, at the end of August, we have snow again, for last night brought the first snowfall of the year. All around me are snow-laden branches.

Every stone has a little white cap on it, with the hush and the silence that snow always gives. Where I am standing in the creek everything sounds clear; every murmur of the brook is to be heard. That was my first impression this morning, the clarity of the sound of the running creek. There's one other sound, for Willow the cat insisted on following me. There she is, needing to be part of it. The weight of snow has flattened the grass, making it difficult to go forward, like the pressure of waves in water. But it is wet snow, and soon will melt.

In my secret spot, and mirrored within its pool, are snow-laden boughs. As I glance up they are above me, and as I glance down they are reflected in the water.

Next day we went again to the woods to listen and watch, and they had never seemed so alive and fresh as they did this time. Another snowstorm was on the way, and the electricity in the air was so interesting. It seemingly lifted all the horses up from the ground. Bucky too had the impulsion of this storm. He buzzed the horses' feet, chasing them with new energy. I could sense the imminent storm in his behaviour. He came inside the house, rolled on his back, and put his head on the sofa for the cat to comb his hair as she does her own. All this within a beat of time. So much activity; they knew it was about to happen. The horses lifted their bodies up, standing on their hind legs as if to quarrel with each other, but they were just whirling and playing with new-found energy before the snowstorm came.

I now know about the Japanese idea of not pulling KI (the Chinese say CHI). This means not to pull your energy towards you, even in this cold. Let it flow. I am breathing. The trees are breathing. The clouds are breathing. The dawn beauty took my breath away into it.

Why should I try to gather it into me and hold it? And feet should flow too: it's better to have "brave feet" than clenched-up ones in this weather. Old riders know when a horse has "brave feet", that is, no fear in him, able to meet the earth.

Now Bucky is grazing the moist grass. Of late he has had many more dreams than I; I wish for a rich dream like the one he has been having.

It's a silent wood, and it throws one back on one's inward happiness. A little bird is chirping behind me. He's heard me, I guess. Is it a bird? No, it's a squirrel. So, squirrel companion, Willow companion, Bucky companion. Each of us taking up our place. But now Willow's decided she needs to go to Bucky to get warm. She's rubbing herself against his hind quarters. Imperial Bucky. He just wouldn't allow her to come close to me right now. He did two steps forward to declare his territory. Then he sat first on one side of me and then on the other.

Poor Willow's feet are cold. I think she got them frozen once in the snow. I have to manage myself on these slippery surfaces. In fact, I tripped once. It's a bit of a restless morning, although it's peaceful; restless because of the change in the weather. Bucky's gone off because he's fed up with my concern for Willow's cold feet. Pussy Willow's pussy feet.

Next day, when Bucky and I set out for a walk in the rain, thinking to leave Willow on the veranda, she decided to accompany us again, for no one likes to be excluded from a party. But when we came to the creek she couldn't cross: it was too deep. So she sat on a big boulder at the water's edge and howled loudly, which was not wise as any coyote could have heard her. She of course won out and we retraced our steps, joined her on her side of the creek, and forgot the previously planned event.

Willow's spiritual presence is as strong as that of an elephant, and she certainly makes that felt, as she did sitting on the boulder.

A few days later, going once again to my secret spot, I thought to find a new tree trunk to sit against, and discovered one with a lacery of twigs, with lichen and moss hanging from them.

I thought to myself this is so much like the spot in the ancient forest in the Arctic where I had been just after a bear had sat. Walking about later in the woods here, very near that chosen tree, I saw some huge scats that could not be a coyote's. I thought they might have been a mountain cat, but luckily that evening Andy appeared and came to track with me. He verified that it was bear manure and quite fresh – two to five days old. So now, unknown to me, a bear had sat and added to the sanctity of my secret spot.

I have just come upon torn-apart animal remains scattered hereabouts that have recently passed through someone's mouth. It looks like a bear.

I chose to have a "bear sit", for I want to draw near the Otherness of the bear. It was as if his element of vitality itself palpably entered my skin. The energy of the earth and his energy came through to me. I could sit on a throne, on a woolsack, on a stuffed sofa, but none would give me the high I feel sitting now where a bear has just sat.

His choice of spot with a long extended branch overhanging the water enabling me to see up and down the creek without being seen is truly a secret spot.

The carriage and the car have caused us to lose our feet, but as children we still had them. It is fun, then, to step into larger footprints. When small I would put on my mother's high-heeled shoes and play being big. Symbolically men have that feeling in business of stepping into larger shoes when vice-presidents become presidents.

In the Now moment I place my small bare foot within the fresh bear paw print. It is awesome and humbling.

He chose, or I chose, the secret spot well, and it has been made more sacred by his being here. Blessed by a bear!

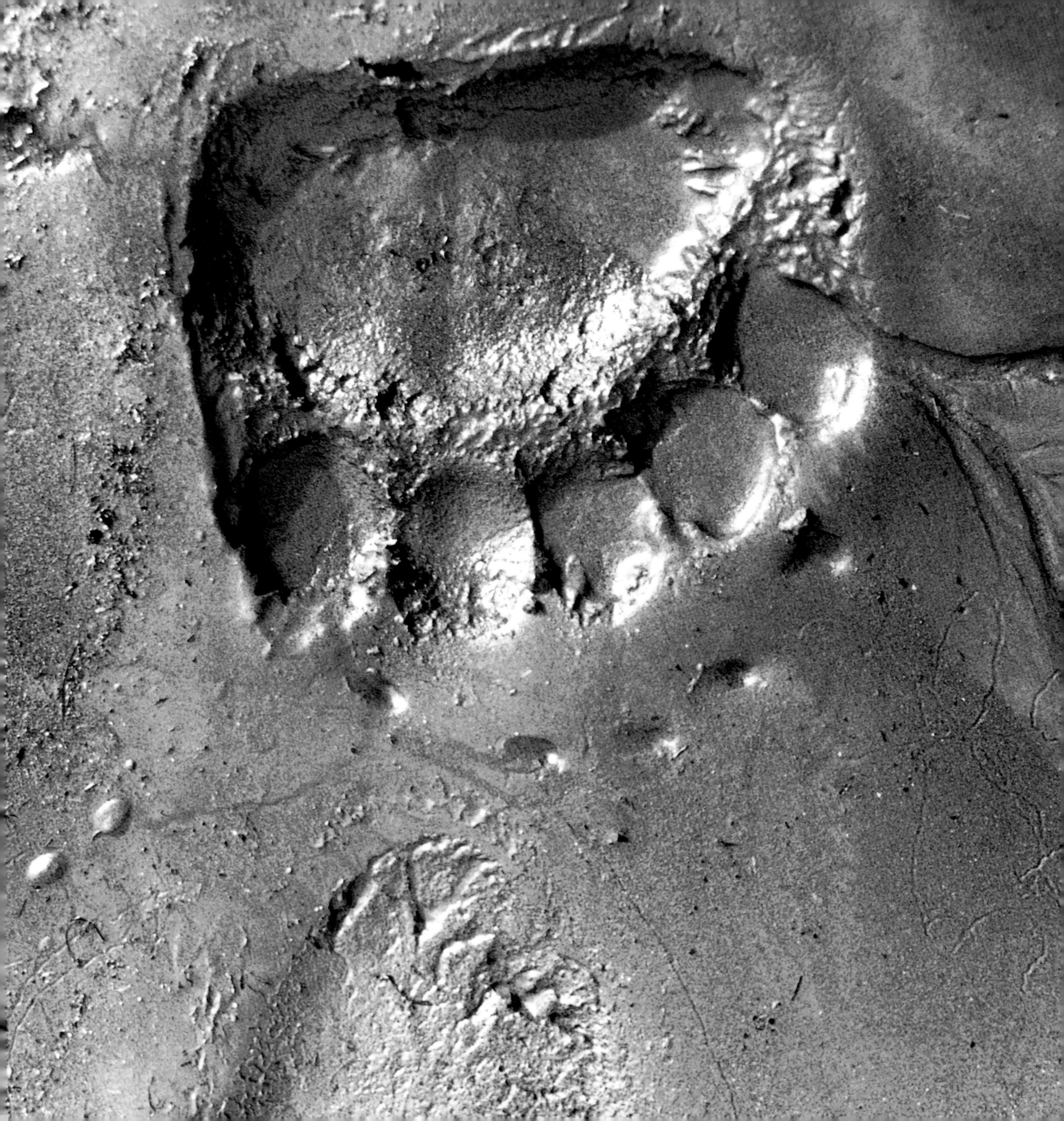

The Essence of Ranching

"Got to give up the iron."

I asked three respected Alberta men – Sandy Cross, Francis Gardner and Dr Bob Church – what they felt to be the essence of ranching.

Francis Gardner said: *"What is the essence of ranching? Ranching can be profit: or ranching can be an oasis or native ecosystems in a desert of change and demand. If we are realistic and visionary to some degree, then we can say ranching sets the stage for primary multi-generational sustainability."*

Dr Bob Church replied: *"I am a steward of the grass and I market through a cow. Grass management comes first, and the cattle fit into that programme. I have tried to develop tougher cattle that eat less. The fall calving programme is a manifestation of this programme. I am in the grass business."*

Sandy Cross's answer was pure poetry: *"Grass is the forgiveness of nature. Her constant benefaction. Forests decay, harvests perish, flowers vanish but grass is immortal…Its tenacious fibres hold the earth in its place, and prevent its soluble components from washing into the wasting sea.*

"It invades the solitude of deserts, climbs the inaccessible slopes and forbidding pinnacles of mountains, modifies climates and determines the history, character and destination of nations.

"Unobtrusive and patient, it has immortal vigour and aggression. Banished from the thoroughfare and the field, it bides its time to return, and when vigilance is relaxed, or the dynasty has perished, it silently resumes the throne from which it has been expelled, but which it never abdicates.

"It bears no blazonry of bloom to charm the senses with fragrance or splendour, but its homely hue is more enchanting than the lily or the rose. It yields no fruit in earth or air, and yet, should its harvest fail for a single year, famine would depopulate the world." (Ingalls)

I want to write about the fashion of change as it affects ranching, and about the rhythm of change that is an essential part of that life.

Ranching today is big business; a ranch costs millions of dollars. Behind the cowboy on his horse "followin' that ol' cow" are the landowners who must bear the fiscal responsibility and possess the skill to understand government regulations and the method of working of the various government departments, banking, accountancy, law, and the suppliers of farm machinery firms. They must also be able to work with and learn from their neighbours.

This is the structure of the ranch – the cattle; the grass they feed on, and the animal husbandry, are the core. Ranching is one-third cattle, one-third grass, and one-third maintenance.

During the Depression the policy was to breed cattle that were very small, as they needed less food. In Scotland the beautiful shorthorn was turned almost into a big poodle. Then came the boom, and after shrinking the poor creatures we wanted to stretch them, for the more pounds in weight gain, the more pennies in one's pocket. So the Australian shorthorn, which had not suffered the fate of the Scottish variety, was imported, as well as some inappropriate European breeds. In other words, during the Depression we wanted mini-cows, and during the boom instant elephants. None of this gave thought to the rightful time needed for evolution.

In a field near my ranch a "cattleman" wished to increase the milk yield of Chianina imported from Italy by introducing into his herd the dairy-breed Holsteins. This was a quick fix, so that the calves, he hoped, would have more milk to suck. But the cross-breeding did not work, and in his field I saw eight dead calves : he had thought of a part, the milk yield, but not of the whole.

It was the large breeds, recently brought in, which were fashionable when I started on my own in the early seventies – Anjou, Simmenthal, Limousin and Charolais. With a grandfather who had homesteaded in Alberta, a father who owned one of the larger outfits in the province, and a veterinarian husband who had the care in his day of the cattle on two big ranches, Burns and Colpitts, land and ranching have always been in my blood and in my being. To all four of us this senseless following of the fashions went against our instincts and our experience. It was one thing when one listened to the breeders of the exotic strains, and quite another when one talked to the men who actually had to do the calving. For the calves were often too large, leading to water on the brain, to aberrant behaviour such as walking in circles, and to mothers who could no longer be motherly but treated their calves as if they were pieces of furniture, to be kicked out of the way.

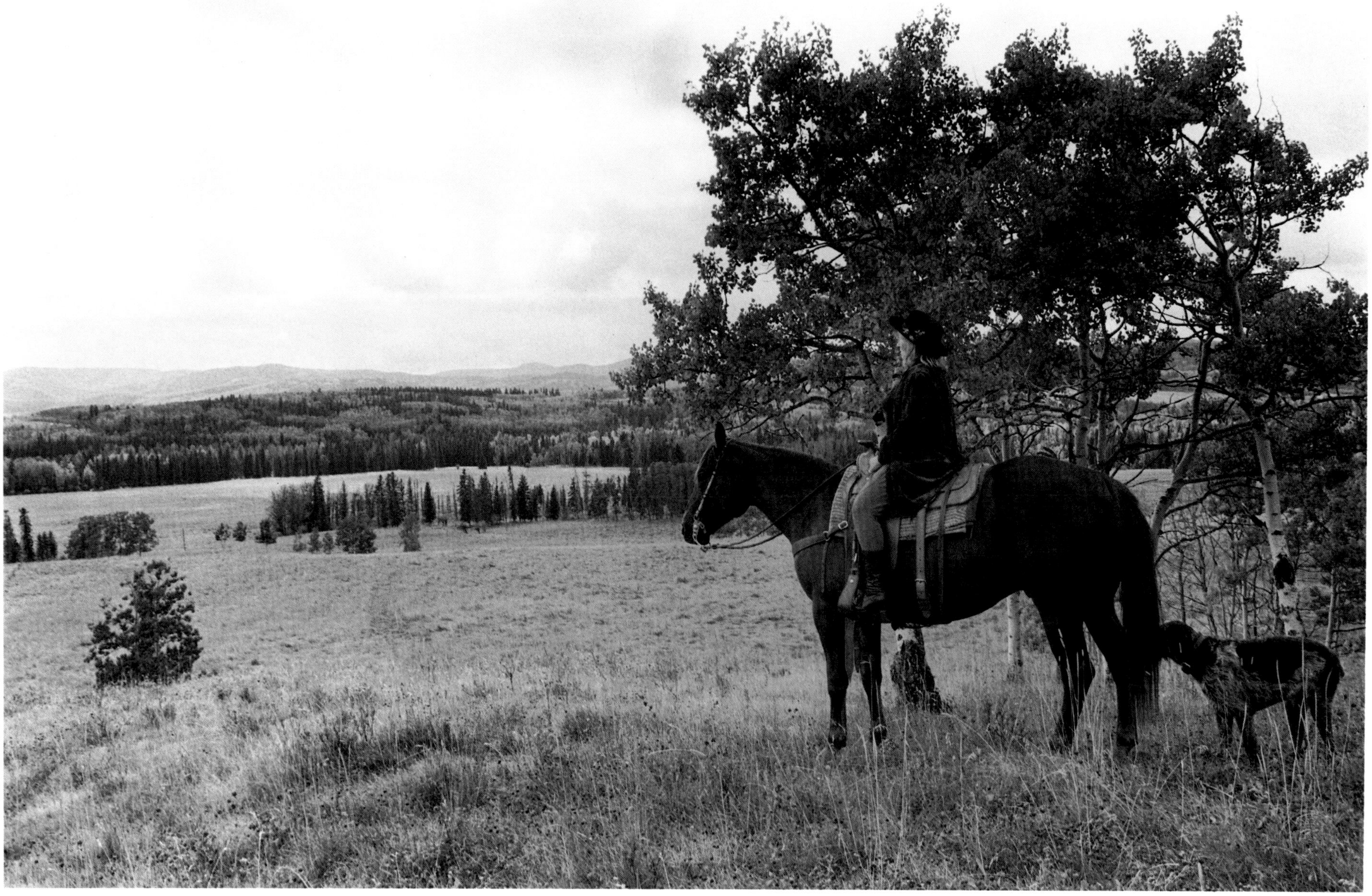

At the other end of the scale there was an attempt at one time to dwarf the Hereford – and in so doing cretins were created. Nor did the breeders pay attention to the fact that in Alberta it is important for the udders to have a dark pigment, since light-coloured udders, in the cold of winter, but with hot sun reflected from the snow, would be very tender.

Sometimes this emphasis just on size, and on the outside of the cow, led to a kind of Alice-in-Wonderland world. In the early seventies, in the best hotel in Calgary, I saw cattle which had been shampooed and hairsprayed taken up in elevators to be auctioned as they stood on carpets and under chandeliers. There was a relationship between the ranchers and their cattle – showy ranchers equated with promoting showy cattle, and quiet ranchers with traditional cattle.

The passion for exotic cows, and for artificial insemination, which expanded at the same time, has pretty well had its day. The latest craze is the scheme to "adopt a cow". These creatures will stay on site and be fed on site, and so the man-link care is gone. The biblical cow and buffalo are now "on shares" to foreign investors who may never actually see the animal in which they have a stake. But the bubble has burst, and some of these breeders are out of business. Somehow the cattlemen were bewitched by the bigness of the cattle, and the old varieties, the British breeds and their crosses, were looked at askance. On my ranch I kept to these true and tried breeds which had been successful with us since the beginning of the century, and which my father and grandfather had bred, but I had many 'phone calls asking me what I was doing with such small cattle and what was my breeding programme. I answered that I looked into the eye of the cow or learned from fellow-ranchers.

There was a fashion too concerning the times of breeding and calving. In Alberta the aim became to calve early in the year, so that the calves would be big for the buyers down east towards the year's end. This policy had nothing to do with the seasons, and calves sometimes died when they were born in twenty below. Now a "ranching for profit" course which I took has come round to the view that perhaps we should calve later, say in May, when there is rich grass which the cow just goes out and eats naturally – and that this is where the profit lies. So after all the ups and downs of trying this and that we come back to the time when nature calves, meaning elk and deer – in May and June.

This conclusion was reached, not by learning from nature but by adding and subtracting the costs of hay, oil, and gasoline for the machines which provided this hay for the cow. So we are back to nature in terms of timing, and we are back to it in terms of grazing, and of following the buffalo's idea of scarifying the soil – grazing hard for a little while and then wandering off for a long time so that the flowers can come back, go to seed and renew themselves. My hope is to create an oasis of terrain where the cow and the buffalo can meet on that indigenous vegetation. The true energy we have as ranchers is the energy of the sun that produces grass. It is much better left uncut for the cattle to browse at the right time.

On some ranches a switch has been made to the buffalo, which in contrast to a cow has a body built like an arrow, wide in front and narrow behind; it can walk into a fire and through it. A cow usually puts her back to the storm and ends up blown into the ditch, whereas the buffalo is able to withstand the rigours of the Canadian winter. John Snow has a small herd at the Stoney Reserve, but white men who try to follow the same path all too often come to grief from lack of understanding and the desire to make money.

Once I saw in my travels an enclosed buffalo who could not forage for what his body needed and was totally dependent on being spoonfed. Insensitively and richly fed on grain unnatural to him, he was crippled within a few years. He had to hide behind other creatures, ashamed of his handicapped way of walking, for instinctively buffaloes know their nobility of movement in nature – to be more inwardly still than we or the cow can be, and yet move like a flash of light when necessary. He is now confined, grain-fed and clumsy. One of the buffalo farmers boasted that his father was in cows for eighty years, and listed all the countless distortions and diseases that man's link with the cow had created. So, according to him, this was the ideal time to return to the buffalo; but it was in his piece of the country that I set eyes on this poor arthritic creature, his crippling brought about not in a hundred years but in three to five.

More recently twenty-six of us sat for eight days, at a conference organised by an American group, trying to work out by mathematics what was most cost-effective in ranching. Two very good ranchers in my group said to one another, "We'll have to give up the iron" –

meaning their big machines. They didn't like parting with their toys, they said, but our calculations had shown that machines did not make accounting sense in terms of cost, depreciation, gasoline, diesel, repairs and time. But why did we have to resort to arithmetic to find out what we had learned through the centuries from nature?

Perhaps common sense is prevailing because, just as the lap-top generals haven't proved to be too clever in war, so the ranchers who talk to each other by computer, and know where their cows are by computer, are too removed from animal husbandry.

There is no substitute for good cowboys such as Jim Commodore and Gordon Heggie, a total gentleman, an elder of his church, father of nine and grandfather of thirty. I have never known anyone truer, or anyone whose horses are quieter. Jim and Gordon understand about health, and quietly, with their cowboy skills, interleave with their herd without stress, thereby creating a climate for a healthy herd and healthy economics.

Destruction of the big ranches has been silent and entire and there are not many left. Every big ranch that has gone down the tube has done so because of the fantasies of men who see themselves as the owners of such ranches. So strong is this dream that it clouds their perception of the land's true needs. They do not understand how much knowledge is required of the care and health and husbandry of cattle, and are dismayed when they meet the envy of those with a smaller patch of land.

I have flown in small planes over northern and southern Alberta, hovering like a bird above the land. I have seen the grass cover after a hundred years of the white man, some of it already showing signs of becoming desert. The grass, once strong, is now limp and has lost its strength. Every machine and every chemical fix has led to alkaline soil or weaker grass. Very rare is the original cover that God meant for this province: very rare is the thick prairie wool that was there to blanket the earth and nourish the buffalo. That wool, when it freezes, keeps its nutrients, so different is it from the tame grass we have unwisely put in its stead, for, when it is grazed after frost hits, it runs right through the cow's body.

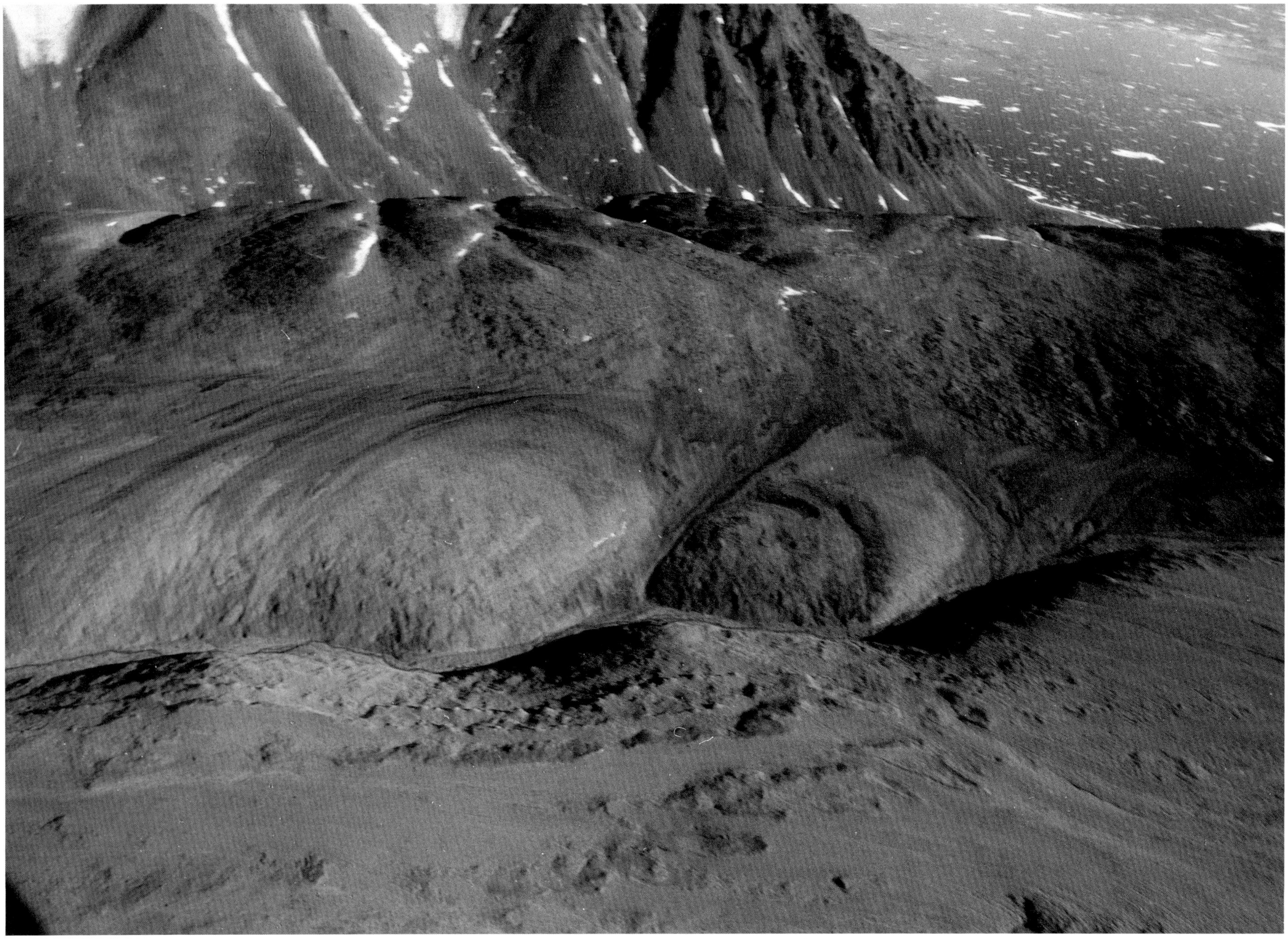

Heraclitus said one cannot step in the same river twice. But did not his disciple add that one cannot put one's foot in the same stream once? We all know of change, the metaphysical element of time and life's movement. Why all this cowtowing to the latest fashion guru on change? We have no right to impose mental empires on each other's thoughts; it puts us into prisons of the spirit that we have created ourselves. Who better than ranchers can make an effort to shift the dead weight of the modern mind which is causing so much suffering?

Nor must we follow the latest trend of ovarian transplants or biogenetic engineering. When we biogenetically engineer mad forms of life, we cannot take them back. The changes are unforeseeable and virtually unstoppable. Why do some scientists not say no? Why do some ranchers not say no? There is no absolution from responsibility; it takes courage to see the truth.

In the past forty years there has been one sacrosanct command — "Thou shalt not impose censorship or restrictions in any circumstances". This philosophy equates liberty with a licence to do anything we want, no matter what the consequences may be. Enthusiasm for launching a new company, a new adventure with venture capital to follow, even if it results in the creation of mad forms of life – all this masquerades as true vitality.

We are asked by Dr Lowell Catlett, Professor of Agricultural Economics and Agricultural Business at New Mexico State University, to visualise a world in which technology will enable doctors to peer inside our brains, or make it possible for us to read *War and Peace* and the Bible on the same day, or digest the fact that "every seventeen seconds a new high-tech product is brought into the market". For ranchers, Dr Catlett proclaims, this means harvesting cow brains by using a DNA or biological computer, leaving technology to take care of crops, spraying pesticides at the behest of a microchip, and implanting medicines in the cattle for slow release at set intervals.

Where are the animals in all this? People in towns are already four or five generations from the Source. Cannot we who live in it as ranchers be conduits of that Source, and therefore gain inner balance and be purveyors today of common sense?

As landowners we perceive an interaction of nature that is not passive. We have the gift and vision of knowing the whole as it is, linking theory and observation, which then leads to that rare commodity – common sense. One can draw universal rules from finite material. There is no beginning to our year, only current patterns on a scroll unwinding. The actions and work of the farmers and ranchers have solemn consequences, because they are performed within a cosmic cycle of the year. Summer and winter, spring seed time and fall harvest build up their essential forms, each with its own significance. We become part of a sphere of holiness; we need only think back to the importance of the rhythm of the seasons in the religious experience of early agricultural societies. It is a life's work that has been part of existence since man and beast were created.

Range men lived in the era largely before fences: they learned to focus on a small calf and yet recognize it as part of infinity.

With a true understanding of rhythm the right quality of change will evolve. To see each creature as an eternal part of the whole gives one a perspective, and does not allow for overreacting to this wave and that group. Crossing the rhythm of life is the real poison of the twentieth century, and we have a role to play in rebalancing it.

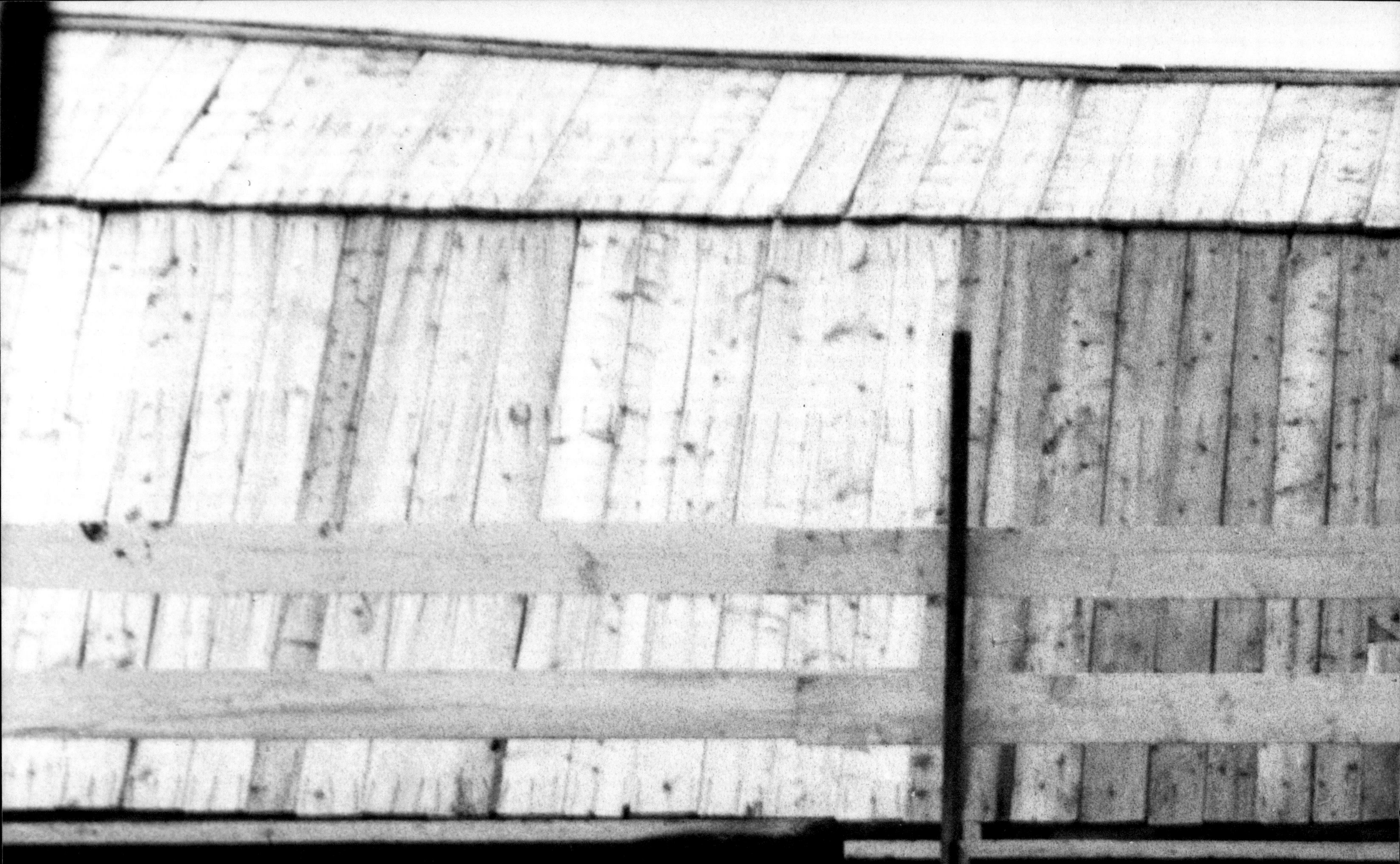

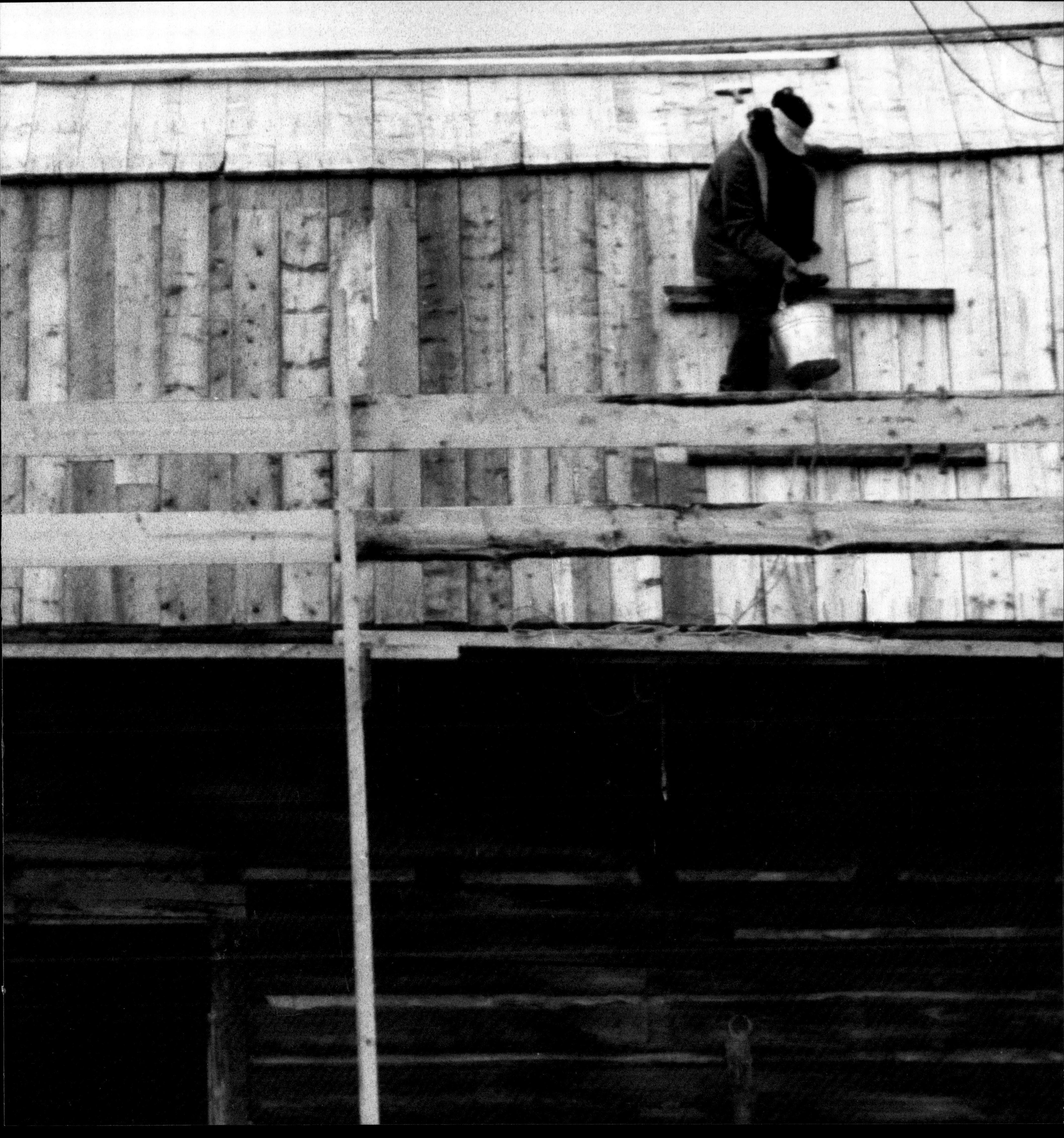

The feverish scurry and flurry of the squirrels' winter work is over, the last stages of preparing for hibernation are done, the last nuts stored.

Now that the squirrels have gone to bed the chickadees have come. I've not seen chickadees all summer, but today three of them are flying from branch to branch, having a quiet look at me. Swinging on the lower branches, sitting on the edges so that they can have a clear view. Flying just above the water, all at very low level this morning so that they can get to know the creature rooted against the tree trunk – me.

I am sitting at the foot of my special tree, with the sun coming through.... It rained last night, and on my tree, at my special spot, every raindrop reveals a rainbow.

Bucky is worrying at something strange in the background, behind all the foliage and trees. He is protecting me from a distance today, not invading my space. Usually he likes to sit and share, but today there is something new and he wants to look at it alone.

Although it is almost mid-October there's still some hithering and thithering between the squirrels' winter homes – they have come out because of the Indian summer. One of them is calling calmly, not with the urgency of preparation that I heard before, "What are you doing here? Who are you? This is my domain."

I sit with my back against the tree, and my body settles into the base of its trunk. The roots of the tree go all the way down to connect energetically with the source of Mother Earth. I only connect with the Great Spirit, but I guess that is a pretty good connection too. A particular comfort and energy come from nestling one's back into the trunk of a tree.

The countless luminous rays of the morning sun reach me through the pine trees. Bucky, having seen and felt the newness of this day too in our wood, has come to huddle and cuddle again so that we can feel it together through the low pine boughs. In the distance I can see a runnel of water with light on it, a lovely surprise, like a secret water spot.

The light and the trickle of the water, the quiet squirrels, all the unseen harmony, bless me with a state of grace.

A ruffed grouse hen sits quietly gazing at me; she was able to skirt safely around Bucky's nose and eyes. The creatures of the wood have become used to me, for my tracks to the tree are part of my daily life.

Sometimes Willow is there before me. Today she's come for a brief visit. She does much more of connecting heaven and earth than I do, for she always enters the little pockets she sees in the earth, and she climbs trees higher than I do. She's found a hole in the forest floor where two old logs have fallen and crossed each other, and at their intersection there's a huge hole. She goes down there to sniff it out, to see whether it's a coyote den or not. Now she comes out and stands on a dead tree trunk near it, having a look about for the deadly enemy, the coyote. After all, one did swallow her aunt, or her grandmother – no, it was her mother. She looks so pretty, walking along the fallen pine tree, and as she gets to one end of the root the other end rises up like a see-saw.

The same God that brought the leaves in spring has blown them away, and the trees are bare. It's lovely to see all the places where the fallen leaves have come to rest, some in branches, some in twiglets, some on the forest floor, others in the water. All in different spots where they have landed for the winter. Soon the wind will come and put them further afield, then time will impinge on them and they will turn into earth. As we go walking home through this wonderful tree canopy, our feet rustle through the new covering of leaves. I love barren trees and barren bushes, preparing for the reception of snow blankets.

I feel at home here, for to me everywhere in the world, except northern parts of Canada, the Arctic and Siberia, Mongolia and the north of Scotland, is suburbs. Nowhere else can you get even a tinge of a feeling of what was before man came. Here and now I am beginning to feel primordial time. Last night and this morning there were elk and coyotes near. What we need are not only human trails but animal trails too, to allow animals to graze again on the indigenous prairie wool that nourished them so well.

Fresh Tracks

At last the time came for me to leave Rumsey. The poison in the mist that rose from the poisoned land contained, at times, biocides that could kill. In winter, when the mist became frozen, it would descend into my house in the form of pink and green fumes. Underneath me were all those pipelines pulling from the earth whatever commodities were wanted; above were fitful gas attacks. Sometimes I had to put my head lower than my body to get oxygen, and I lost feeling in my extremities – exactly, I was told, the symptoms produced by breathing in neurotoxins. Most people left, but I was intoxicated with the injustice of good air becoming bad air. When I was told that the new plant was efficient, I merely saw it as a super-efficient gas chamber. What happens to the earth happens to us all. So what was once my Garden of Eden became a company quarry.

My dream, my new Eden, was to have native grass again with indigenous creatures roaming on it, where there would still be reverence for the one who created all. For a long time I travelled Canada's vast territories, seeking land. At last I found it, on the ranch of John Cartwright, who belongs to one of Alberta's respected ranching families.

Wanting him to know what was important to me, I decided to share with him the little forest that hid my secret spot. He said that he too had an enchanted forest which he would show me one day.

With great gusto, I proceeded to be the guide. I wished to take him to a quiet glade of evergreens whose feet were still embedded in an ice-field, for it was dense and dark in this part of the woods, keeping them much further back into winter than the rest of the ranch. To reach them I had to cross a frozen gully, and he, gazing thereon with more expert eyes, said, "It is deep", but I didn't want to hear. He looked warily and quietly and did not stir. I like meeting danger, and, although the dark blue water was peeping through, I tested with one foot close to the other, inching along with the reassuring words, "It's all right, it's all right", with each sidestep. When I was three-quarters across he dared to begin, the ice broke, and we both, hardly knowing each other, stood stunned face to face in cold black water. I was up to my armpits, he to his waist. He was way taller and bigger than I was, and I looked at him and said, "You'll have to help me". He was able to exert leverage with his foot against the edge and get to the other side, and when he was grounded he pulled me up and out.

He emptied his duck boots and I my gum boots, but these were futile emptyings because all our clothes were sodden and continued to leak. But, like children who test danger, we became close without words.

With kindness and generosity, a contract was drawn up and signed with mutual trust, sealed by an old-fashioned Alberta handshake.

The following spring and summer were my last at Rumsey. The black water hole which had engulfed us a year earlier was now dry, with just a touch of ice at the bottom, and a total tangle of roots. It was a standing of dead wood, for the oil company had changed the course of the water. And right in the hole where I had fallen in with John Cartwright there was a bear track, though I could hardly believe what I saw. The only track I had ever seen here other than a coyote's belonged to a bear. I saw it once, and now before my eyes was a second one. It made sense that a bear would like this hole, for it was a nice one to be in.

The next day the house where I had lived for twenty-four years was to be moved to my new land. It was 3pm on a Saturday, and the sun was going down. The tips of the tree tops were aglow with the sunset light, but down at the base of the trunk it was dark. I was in the dusk, but linked up with the radial axis of the setting sun, piercing through the fir forest with the diamond glow that flows from it. I looked into the eye of the sunset and it looked into mine; after that, with the prism of light in my eyes closed or open, I saw beautiful green and blue sunspots.

Beneath my tree I sat and felt the earth, for there was a spirit in the woods. One can hear the grass growing, but in this living silence I felt a sense of pain, an awareness of the invasion, soon to take place, of the new, carefully selected purchaser who – I was sure – would not be an environmentalist or a tree hugger. The cloudy sky was letting go its rain in sympathy with my sadness.

Of course, all the animals, all the wild life, had fled with the ploughing of the new people. I had watched them the day before, flapping about fixing a machine, fiddling with this and that, unaware – as they will always be – of the hidden magic of this land.

Although I leave, the trees and animals cannot. They must remain to meet the new onslaught. I go with my memories, and hear, far off in the future, the unfamiliar cries, the unrecognised sounds that they emit when cornered. Here the air is polluted, the oil Plant gives off noise, and now also there are the voices of animals in fear.

Could one have foreseen it? The land and animals could not have done so, for oil men have their strange ways. Grief, this new grief, has its surprising ways too.

Somehow I shall stand the test. I felt the warm rustle of leaves, like a feast day, a holy day, which each day on this earth is. All the earth is our inheritance, to share with All.

Huge gusts of wind assailed the land. There was a great swaying in the woods, deep from the roots to the tops of the trees, and I thanked God for their strong-rootedness. It was as if they were swaying whilst praying. The Old Testament and the Natives tell us that God is in the wind, and one of the Hebrew words for "soul" is "wind". Trunk to top there was a swaying and I was in it. It was exciting and frightening at the same time, but it had a rhythm. This was my past. The Natives, when moving from a camp ground they especially liked, would leave strings of beads or little pouches behind, as a gift to the place. I too have left behind a symbolic offering of gratitude.

I said goodbye to my long-standing pine trees. The trunks seemed dead, but lichen covered the skeletons of their lower branches. And I visited a strong tree couple I knew. Pine trees mostly stand alone, or in groups, yet here was a couple, male and female, joined together as in marriage.

Next day my house had gone, carried on a trailer to its new site. When it moved, the squirrel that inhabited the roof ran back and forth along the cedar shingles. The movers told me that it ran from side to side during the whole of the journey, and then went off at the cattle guard of the new ranch. We hope to see it again one day soon.

After the house had left, I went with Bucky to his special hill. The house was somehow meant to move, for Bucky's hill, his viewing hill of the coyotes, was more permanent than the house I had built. His sixth sense was mindful of the move: he had marked repeatedly all the contents of the building, but still it went down the road, which he couldn't understand, because when he marks trees they don't move. His hill will always be there and my house will not.

It is strange to look at the remains of the house you once lived in. It's very interesting — almost exhilarating — to see the ethereal quality of everything; it really makes you understand that the numinous is more important than the material. Usually people move on, but I've been able to move and also to look back, and "feel back" at the same time as I'm going forward.

I needed a new road for my virgin land, and one of the crew of four who made it was called Rollinmud. He told me that, in coming, he felt he was returning home, for he had rolled down these hills as a child.

I learned from him that not only were the buffaloes and cows "drawn" here for shelter, but that this was the wintering ground of the Natives. Rollinmud showed me where the teepees had been, and where his ancesters were buried. As on the Nile, they lived on one side of the creek and were buried on the other. Then Bearspaw came and put up new teepees for me. Together, making peace with the Ancestors' spirits, we have fenced in the burial sites and scattered wild flower seeds over them.

And now I am in the foothills of Alberta, with a glad heart. There is good air here, and oddly it has a way of carrying you on. The grass is as God intended it to be, a blanket cover for the earth and forage for its inhabitants. It is bear country, where every big stone has been upended so that the bears can eat the delicious ants underneath. Even the bugs are wilder here.

At Rumsey I took grass that was billiard-ball smooth with over-grazing, and in twenty-four years I restored it, only to see the bush apes plough it up, let it blow, graze it down to nothing, and be so profligate in the use of hay, just throwing it about, letting animals stamp or lie on it, that afterwards they wouldn't eat it. I suppose some would say I might as well not have tried — who really knows?

The house feels happy where it now is. The siting is beautiful. I look up to shoulders of the glacial field which fills the whole circumference of my glance. To know that everything around and underneath has been from prehistoric times as unaltered as the stars overhead gives ballast to the mind.

Pekisko Creek, my creek, changes, the towns change, the people change, yet the land remains.

Along with the Natives John Cartwright's father, Jim Cartwright is buried here. His shadow lies flat and still but his spirit spreads out and is very strong in these surroundings. He is bound by countless ties of love and thought to everything on this part of the earth.

Sitting beside the running stream in this Indian summer sunset light I could see the shimmering, trembling water that had once reflected Jim Cartwright as he rode across it.

They tell me he did his thinking alone on a horse, and the colder the air the more he cared for his cows. His son could testify to that; tucked in close to his father on the saddle, his feet froze at the 40° below that no six-year-old could withstand. Environment was not a word in his time, but he *knew*. He took care of the range, knowing that if you do not pay attention to your country the cows will not do anything for you. They tell me he was conscious of what the water was doing and the grass was doing, and that he took better care of his outfit than most people; the water and pastures offered a glowing tribute to him.

To keep a ranch takes a lot of doing. The women have to be right and the following generation have to be grounded. In older countries the law of primogeniture works for continuity. We have what is clumsily called "inter-generation dilution", meaning that the same land becomes divided between many children. Let us hope there is not a dilution of common sense here.

The Natives, followed first by a homesteader who came and went, and then by Jim Cartwright, all met this patch. Now I, a third generation Albertan, live here.

A man is a centre for nature, running out threads, linking through everything fluid and solid. There is a thread between Jim Cartwright and myself. I feel with this man, whom I have not met, connected with his deep pain denied.

Tracks are outward signs of inward grace. Tracks can be the tangible presence of our soul. Jim Cartwright's soul left his track.

When Jim Commodore came to visit, he said he liked this camp better than the last one. As we stood together, we remembered this land and its past. To come to me one goes over two glacial terraces, with hollows where the cows almost disappear, though they are still happily grazing. The glacial terrain has its benefits, too, because of its hard base, and even though it may be snowed or rained on my car will not sink or wallow in mud.

I sense the impingement on virgin land, and feel a deep sense of responsibility for it. I have made a small trail in laying a winding path. You wind your way to the river-bed, and in this river-bed are rocks of the Jurassic Period, which a geophysicist has told me made this land that I am on, in the glacial period, the shore of the ocean. Where my grandparents homesteaded at Rumsey was dinosaur land, and in those days was the actual ocean.

As we stood at the creek, Jim Commodore said that it was to this place, known to the cowboy as the Draw, that all the cows came during the winter period before fences. Cowboys had to travel from as far away as Cochrane, about fifty miles distant, to claim their herds, so you see the necessity of the brand. This was prime wintering ground; at the beginning this was where the buffalo came for shelter in snowstorms, and this is where I now abide.

Sweet smell of earth and air, good-tasting water. I enter my teepee to the fourth element – fire.

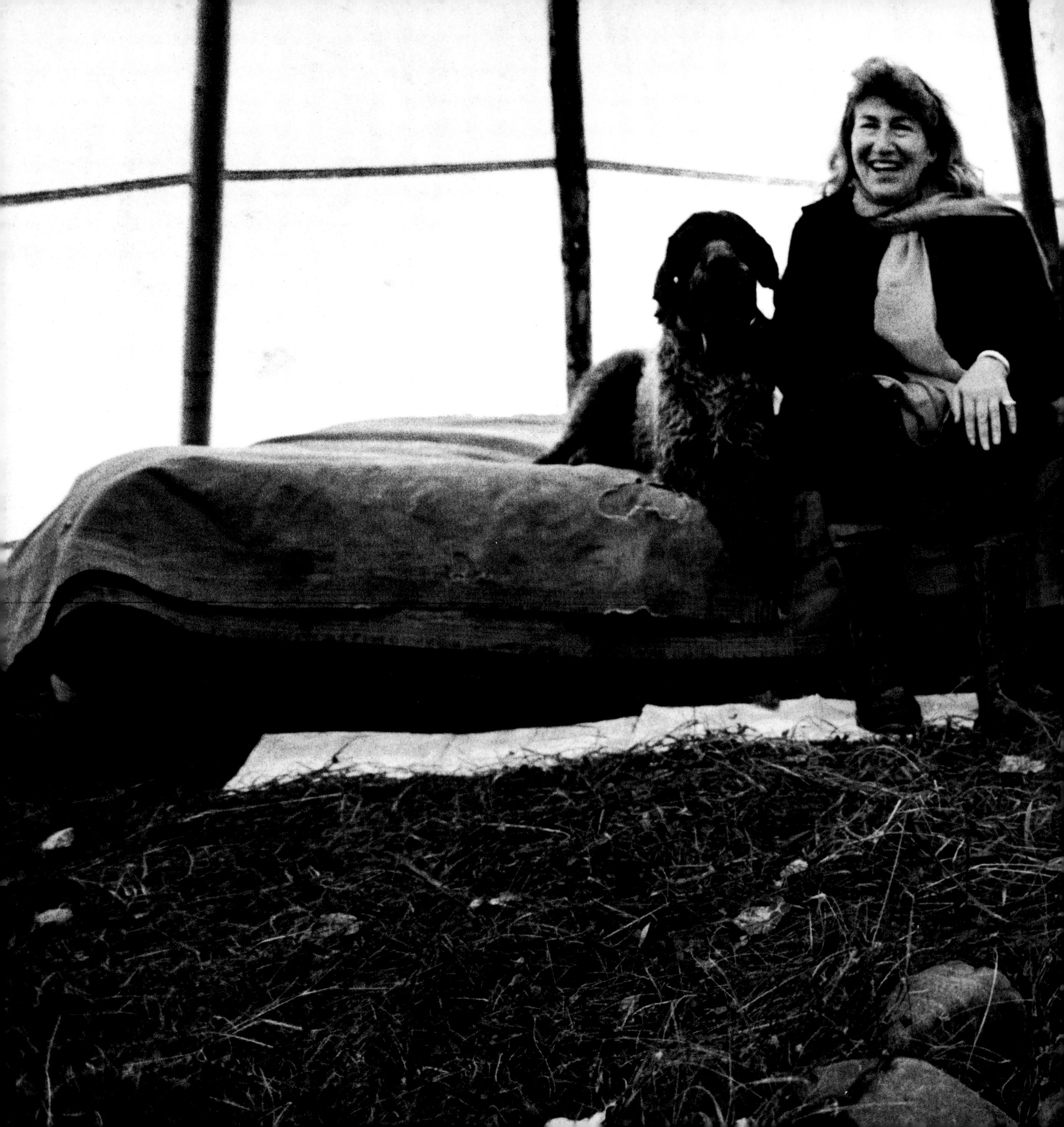

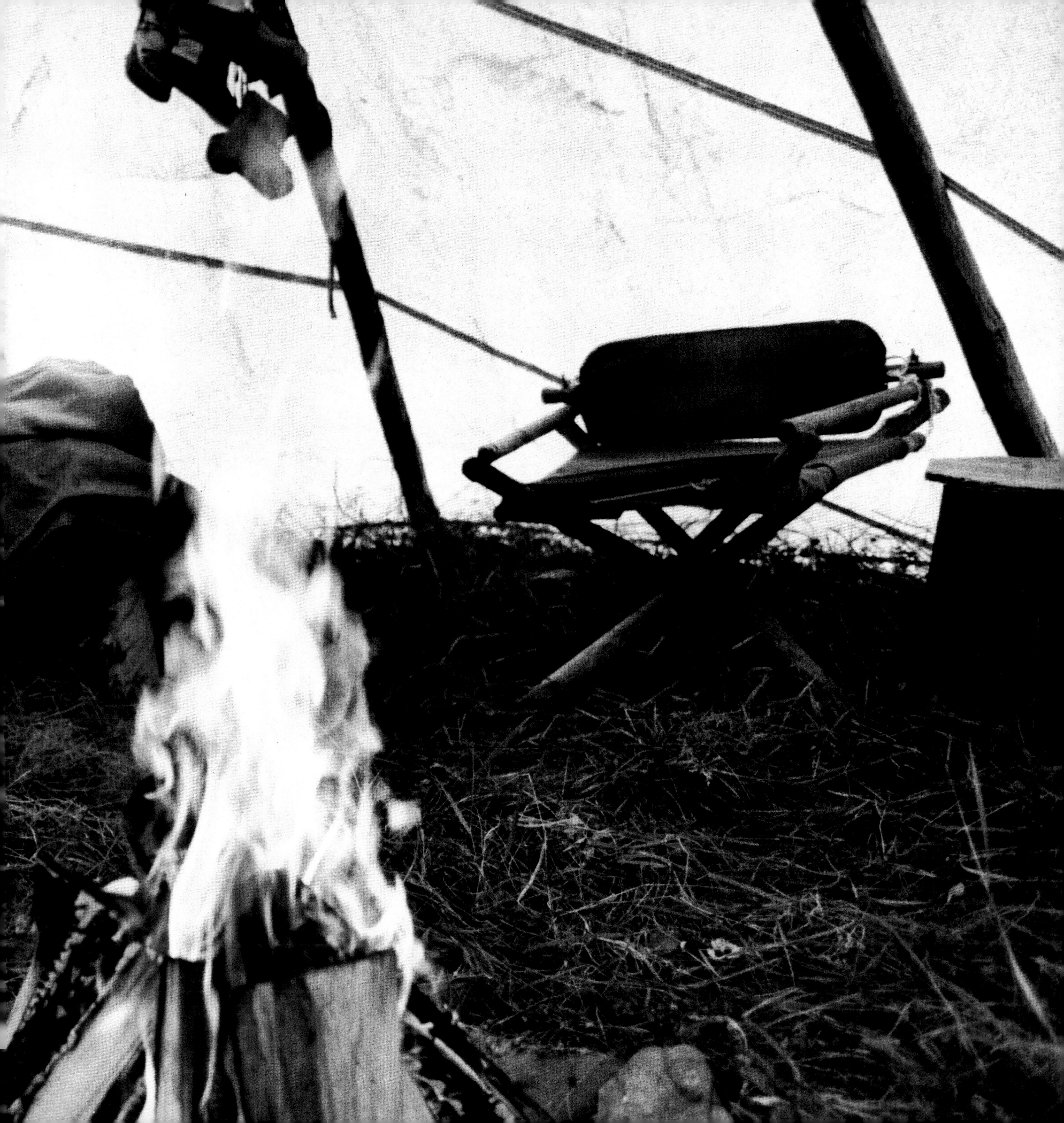

Before the break of day, lying in bed I heard a much-too-early chorus of ravens, and with it the howl of coyotes; a change in the customary rhythm of light and the sounds that accompany the rising of the sun. I knew then that some creature had died and that there was great excitement and anticipation in the air. The unusual sounds at that hour tugged at me, and I had to figure them out.

I set off and crossed the creek to the silence of the place where the Natives are buried; the quiet is even greater there. A cow had slipped off the bank, aborted, and died, and in the frost was a fresh carcass. One could feel the pain she had endured, and hope it had not lasted long. The coyotes and ravens had already begun feasting.

Bucky, seeing bird and animal tracks in the snow, began doing his favourite thing – coyote tracking. He was so intensely excited about this chase that when I called him back he had to go the full round of a racecourse before he could slow down and stop.
So elemental was the spirit of the hunt that although he nodded to me he was off again in hot pursuit. Soon the coyotes were howling at him and he was barking back at them, and I was yelling for fear of his being overtaken and outnumbered. So we had a three-part cacophony: their and Bucky's screams and howls, and mine. It seemed there was no one to listen, but if someone from above was doing so He might have smiled.

A day or two later, before dawn had broken, with the snow conditions just right, I went for an early morning cross-country ski. Bucky criss-crossed my path as I skiied, and Willow, hiding in a tree, watched me as she waited for us to come back. The moon had not yet set, and on the white snow it gave enough light to see where I was going. Leaning on my ski poles, in the purity of the snow, all and everything upwelled. There I stood, waiting in the woods, as two and then three ravens encircled me. I love the silent whirr of their wings which can be heard once they stop their talk.

The day before I had seen their wing prints in the snow, just on the other side of the creek; they looked like angel wings. The ravens had been walking between the cow pats buried in the snow, picking out pieces of grain so as to balance their diet which had been a dead cow feast.

Looking down the creek through the entanglement of growth, I could see a wonderful branch that had fallen across it and sprouted little branches that went straight up like trees. And then there were all the shapes by the edge of the water. There's wasn't one straight line in the rocks alongside the creek. How, then, can we think that the linear way is "the" way or the only way? Bucky and Willow are not formed in straight lines.

Skiing done, we begin our three-creature parade back home, Bucky, Willow and I. Snowy hillsides, slippery hillsides, are much easier for four-footed creatures than for me, and the only solution is to turn into a four-footed creature for a moment. It worked – with only two feet one slithers down. I've just been hit in the face by a great plop of snow. It came down on me, but it was quite pleasant. And now the three of us are going back with all our shared experiences. I thought an owl had jumped off one of the branches, but no, it was just the movement of the snow melting and falling down. It was like a wave in the branch. A sea wave.

I've come back home, but Bucky appeared later, just appeared. Although I offered him a chance to be dry and warm indoors, for he was totally drenched, he looked at me as if to say, "Come on out and have some more fun".

A creature feels at home being drenched by the elements, and does not always need to be dry and warm.

Abide still, O my people, and take thy rest,
for thy quietness shall come.
Nourish thy children, O thou good nurse;
stablish their feet.
Esdras II

Foot of Man and Hoof of Beast

I began this book by inviting you to take a journey into a landscape and the people and creatures thereon, travelling slowly, "for, as with a herd and young calves, if men should overdrive all the herd will die. So I will lead you softly on, according to the pace of the cattle."

I chose the moment of entry to my land, doing what horses and cattle and most creatures love to do – heading for home; I asked you to come back with me to a feeling of Beginnings, and then traverse a continuum of space to sense the Unseen Harmony. All through my book there are tracks, animal tracks and man tracks. Every living thing makes tracks. Leaf fossils in rocks are there for ever; mushrooms leave their spores; salmon making their way upriver to spawn know where to go – that is also a track. In the twentieth century I suppose human tracks are our genetic coding. Tracks are the signature of the soul, the outward sign of inward grace. How evanescent they are; and yet they are the way for us to be connected with creation. Those before us have walked on this landscape, and those of the human species probably left behind mental imprints too. Others to come will also make tracks. May there still be something underfoot, other than pavements or dead earth.

Men today like skiing straight down the mountain side, the faster the better, driving a car for hours and then queueing for hours so that they can ski down in a flash. I prefer leather boots and wooden cross-country skis which you wax according to the temperature of the snow, so that you feel an interleaving with fresh snow crystals before the wind and the elements pack them down; this allows me to listen to what is underfoot even with my gear on. Not so with the present-day downhill outfitting. They are at the opposite pole, consisting of huge, rigid, plastic boots, affixed to equipment designed solely for speed, going faster and faster, on skis as in life.

We have travelled together over this piece of earth with all its tame and untame creatures and men. As I walk on the range, I feel with Wendell Berry that, "What I stand for is what I stand on". I hope that all of us may be able to get away from the skimming of the earth's surface and the scurrying we do over it, and allow our feet in walking to listen to the world below.

Only when we are truly on our feet and truly listening are we in the pure present, or as in the Wisdom of Solomon, "When a bird hath flown through the air, there is no token of her coming to be found, but the light air, being beaten with the stroke of her wings, and parted with the violent noise and motion of them, is passed through, and therein. Afterwards no sign of where she went is to be found." So with us. If we walk down the street and look back, we see nothing to mark our passing.

We ourselves, clad in boots, and in our constant great hurry, often jar with the landscape. The Natives have been in harmony with it, so their tracks on the earth were like gentle streams of narrow footpaths. When they walked or sun-danced or held a pow-wow their wild animals were wandering near them. The earth is moving and we are too. We must move as with the earth's metaphysical element of time.

One of the wise queries of Jim Commodore's philosophy goes like this: "Why is it that whenever the oil man comes into the country, people stop waving to each other?" He noted the respect for human dignity given by the rancher, which is so different from the code of the oil industry. Again, he said of himself that he was content in mid-life, for he had travelled with his horse over every hill he had yearned to get to know. The cowboy rancher fits loosely into the idea of nomad.

What is the source of this wandering? There is a recognition of the part of our species that was born to migrate as animals do. From the beginning of the human race, people have roamed the earth according to their seasonal needs, seeking grazing for their flocks, hunting antelope and buffalo and other animals for their food, picking berries in summer to preserve for later use, and finding shelter in winter. Even people in prisons and animals in zoos, it is noted, have a greater restlessness at what would have been migratory times.

The nomad in me goes back to the desert – to the Bible people and their wandering, and to the love of the land which was always with them. The Stoney Chief told me that the Natives and the Hebrews know this, and the environmentalists are beginning to understand. He pitied the rest. He had never met a Hebrew, but had read the Bible, and he honoured me by including me in an ecumenical conference of eighty of his people from all over North America. They had built a medicine wheel connecting their reservation with the whole world.

The earth is linked with the heavens and the heavens with the earth, the rain and the wind connect them; rain falls to the land and land mists rise to the heavens. In allowing ourselves to feel with our feet the earth rhythms, we become consciously part of creation. The crown of the tree links with the heavens, its roots with the earth, and the trunk of the tree is the bridge between the two. Our feet and our head can be like the crown and the roots, with our body akin to the trunk. Only if we are truly rooted in the earth can we be linked with the heavens.

At this moment I see a buck standing in the wood listening with his hoof. Could we get in touch again with our alertness, which animals have and which once we must have had?

One day I was browsing through a French/Esquimaux dictionary, and I found that in the French column under *marcher* there was only one word for the English *to walk*, but in the Eskimo column there were countless words. Some designated walking as a young man walking, as an old man going on all fours, walking at the head of a group, at the tail of a group, etc. There were no words to describe our tramping and traipsing, which is not listening with one's feet, but is aimless and can be destructive. Some vegetation takes a long time to evolve, and if we are not respectful of how we meet it our footprints can leave oozing wounds.

I try to meet the sanctity of life, the earth and its vegetable kingdom and the creatures thereon. How can we do this if not by establishing our feet first and listening through them while walking? If you stand on the road you feel one thing, and if you stand on the humble grassy ditch beside it you feel something else, a more complete person.

Paths connect man to nature and men to each other, but roads only connect commerce. In Alberta the streets and small towns are empty of people. Cars park, their drivers pick up groceries and animal feed; it is in and out of cars and trucks we go. Trucks are called "pick-ups", and in this pick-up, at the press of a button, music blazes out twenty-four hours a day. In a bigger town, not mine, I sometimes walk in silent wonder at the legs going resolutely nowhere in both directions.

Let us learn from the First People all over the earth.

In years gone by, when Natives sought food, some plants and meat were always left for insects and other creatures. The Stoney Chief told me that when they gathered at sunrise, say, bergamot (horse mint), with six mauve flowers on a plant, they would collect three for themselves and leave three for the bees. When they hunted, they would leave little pieces for little animals, and when they uprooted a plant to use the root for their medicine they would take a pinch of tobacco from their pouch and put into the earth, cover it, and say a prayer of gratitude.

As I travelled up north, in Yukon, Alberta and British Columbia, I saw the range of the buffalo. In a world before fences, the Natives roamed and the buffaloes roamed. As the Natives could range from hunting and eating caribou one season to fishing for salmon along the coast the next, so the buffaloes could travel to find sedge grass that still stood strong, pushing through the snow cover. In a year of wandering, they could find the necessary supplements and minerals in balance for themselves, and even their own salt supply.

We saw a change in the Native when he was put on reservations and his good protein diet gone in a minute. Similarly, once we contain the noble buffalo, and inhibit his wandering and foraging, we have the responsibility to be mindful of the mix of his many needed nutrients. A good cowboy or buffalo boy makes sure in rotating the grazing that his creatures do not run out of "groceries".

Each contour of the earth has a different musical phrase. A profoundly deaf musician, Evelyn Glennie, found the silences on a Scottish rocky island deafening. If a deaf person can find the resonances off rocks deafening, how much more eloquent is the silence from our prairies, our foothills and our northern icelands.

The first people of Australia, who were also nomads, mapped their continent in terms of songlines, which were used to establish territory just as birds define territorial boundaries by their song. As Bruce Chatwin writes, "The contour of the melody of the song described the contour of the land with which it was associated." Songlines were pathways; "song maps" of these trails gave forth the memory of ancestors' footprints, and there was not a creek or a rock that did not have its own tune and rhythm. So, whilst walking in the outer world, the Aborigines became a vessel for the inner world. That which is out there is in fact inside us all the time, if we allow ourselves to listen.

In the words of Kathleen Raine,

Such woods I dream-walked
Age-old, abandoned paths untrodden
By those who were and will not be again.
I trespassed where the trees remember
The ruined dead, who in me imagine
The beauty of their lost domain.

In standing on my land, there is a sense of the Beginning, the innocence of the world and the heart of pure stillness. When one goes out of time and space, wondrous things happen. So listen now to the sounds of the earth, listen with your feet so that you hear and feel this world. We can do so in a park, in our minds, or in bed or hospital. Everyone has a favourite memory of a countryside. Just imagine standing on it in stillness; from that any winging we do will have roots.

The transitions between dawn and day, twilight and night, wood and meadow, trees and grasslands, are vulnerable, so the delicacy in going from outer to inner being is a fragile moment.

When a man steps out of his house in the country he is the same man; when he steps out of his house in a big city he often has to put on a mask – he is a different man. In Rumsey it was possible to go deeply into one's private space and at the next moment into the open wild. Jim Commodore would say at times, "I'm going to shut 'er down", meaning he would close the door, pull down the blinds and not be disturbed. Or else he would go on horseback and ride into the woods, into the open and free. Andy could delve into his imagination and then go off tracking. In a totally urban environment we are never really private, and even when we go into open spaces barriers are erected because of terrorism and vandalism. If we can reach inmost to the totally private and outmost to the totally open and reconcile these two, we have something.

How lucky I am to have sacred meals of wild mushrooms and wild herbs and liturgical sounds out of time in Alberta, in a world as it came straight from the Creator's hands, fresh, pure and strong. In town, too, to live near the centre of one's being is equivalent to living as close as possible to the Gods. The land I had to leave suffered some of the horrors of pollution, but for me it still has the purity of beginnings that I keep in my spirit.

Could industrialists envision the land of Alberta and the creatures that were there in earlier times? Would they then work with the respect due to these animals and plants, designing their facilities to mingle with the elements? Let there not be a final stroke of havoc to the buffalo, the elk and the trees.

Hearing from the wind clouds above our heads the greatest truth on earth, sensing through seasons in their most severe and their most soft, summer and winter, the intimacy of man's remotest beginnings, with the animals and plants and trees we can feel a part of the family of the universe.

When you stand on the earth in the "Now" moment, experiencing the immediacy of the living truth, you are in your own special within and forever, and then you feel a sense of having been known all along by the Creator.

The task of the artist is to sense more keenly than others the harmony of the world, the beauty and outrage of what man has done to it, and poignantly to let people know. In failure as well as in the lower depths – in poverty, in prison, in illness – the consciousness of a stable harmony will never leave him.

Solzhenitzyn

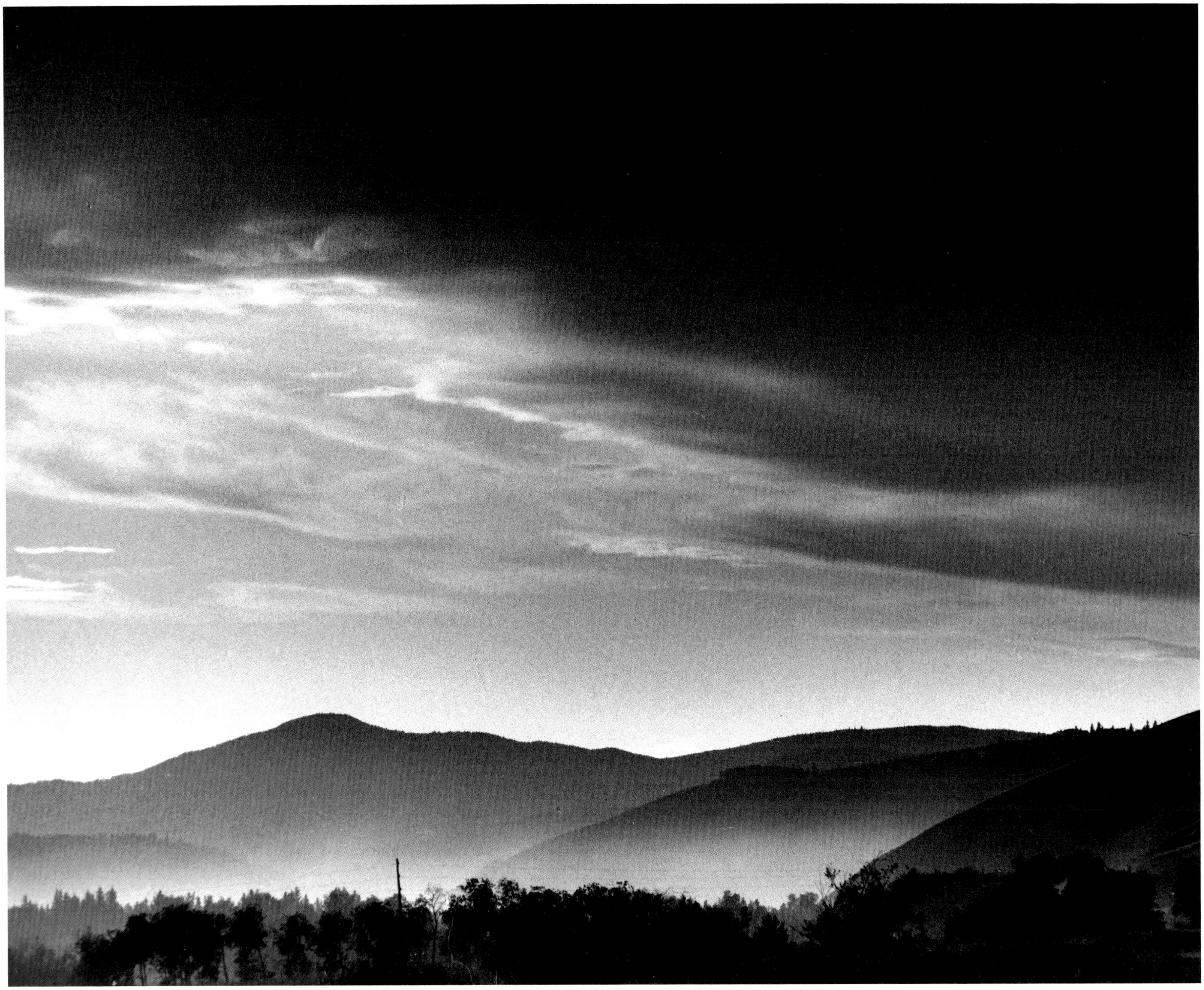

First published 1995 in association with The Book Guild Limited, Lewes, Sussex

Copyright © Zahava Hanan 1995
The poem on page 129 is reproduced by kind permission of Kathleen Raine
All rights reserved
Photographs by Patrick de Marchelier & Zahava Hanan
Off-the-Road transportation: Richard Pullen

Edited by Sheila Bush
Designed by Derek Birdsall RDI
Typeset in Monotype Walbaum by Shirley Birdsall
Production supervised by Martin Lee/Omnific
Printed on Parilux matt cream (an acid-free, dioxin-free recyclable paper) by Balding + Mansell
Bound by Smith Settle

Printed in England

ISBN 0-9697600-5-1